EPIC ACTIONS
OF THE FIRST
WORLD WAR

EPIC ACTIONS
OF THE FIRST
WORLD WAR

R. W. Gould
M.B.E.

Tom Donovan

BRIGHTON

First published in 1997 by
Tom Donovan Publishing Ltd.
2 Newport Street,
Brighton,
East Sussex BN2 3HL

ISBN: 1-871085-39-X

Desk-top typeset by Tom
Donovan Publishing Ltd. Design
and layout by DAG Publications
Ltd, London. Printed and bound
in Great Britain by The Bath
Press, Bath.

Author's Acknowledgements
My thanks to Tom Donovan,
Gordon Griffin, Jim Rooke-
Matthews, Bob Scarlett, Keith
Tranmer, Brian Turner and last,
but certainly not least, the staff
of Goodmayes Library, London
Borough of Redbridge.

A note about the illustrations
The various portraits, drawings,
photographs and maps in this
book have largely been drawn or
adapted from regimental histories
and other contemporary
accounts, or are from private
collections or, in the case of the
service medals were commissioned specially for this work.

Dedicated to the P.B.I.
of the Great War

The other Arms – artillery, engineers, cavalry and
corps – had casualties and brave men aplenty, but only the
men who went 'over the top' armed with a rifle and bayonet
earned for themselves the rueful title of the P.B.I. –
the Poor Bloody Infantry!

Contents

CONTENTS

Foreword

The epic actions mentioned in this book, and there are many more which could have been included, generally deal with units, often isolated, which fought to the last man or bullet. Engagements where battalions, over a short period, were fed time and time again into the mincing machine or near continuous battle (which all but destroyed the British Expeditionary Force [B.E.F.] in 1914) have been excluded. Typical of the 'mincing' process was the fate of the 1st Battalion, the Queen's (Royal West Surrey) Regiment which disembarked in France on 13th August 1914 with a strength of 27 officers, 50 warrant officers and sergeants, 42 corporals and 879 private soldiers, totalling 998 all ranks. Over the next ten weeks six reinforcements of over 500 officers and men joined the battalion. By 1st November 1914, during the first Battle of Ypres, the 1st Queen's was commanded by a subaltern, Lieut. Boyd, with the transport sergeant as his second-in-command. The other ranks consisted of two corporals and 30 privates, which number included the cooks, grooms and orderlies.

Another example is that of the 2nd Battalion, The Prince of Wales Volunteers (South Lancashire) Regiment which landed in France on 14th August 1914 with 27 officers and 980 rank and file. The unit went into action on the 24th at the Battle of Mons and five days later mustered 14 officers and 405 other ranks. During first Ypres, despite reinforcements which were urgently needed (for the regiment lost 148 killed and double that number wounded on just one day, 31st October) the strength had dropped to ten officers and 298 rank and file. By 17th November 1914 the 142 survivors were regrouped into two weak companies, each commanded by a sergeant-major. Their Commanding Officer was the medical officer, Captain Pirrie, R.A.M.C., the only member left of the officers' mess.

Even unluckier were the officers and men of the 2nd Battalion, The Royal Scots Fusiliers, who left their peace time station in Gibraltar and did not land in France until 6th October 1914. Three weeks later during the Battle of Gheluvelt the last few dozen officers and men, including the latest reinforcement of 25 other ranks which had only reached the front line during the previous night, were overwhelmed on 30th October and the battalion ceased to exist.

There are other epic actions lost to history simply because no one was left alive to record what happened. For instance, on 23rd April 1917 during the Battle of Arras the 51st (Highland) Division was attacking eastwards towards Roeux and the Chemical Works some 1000 yards north of the town. 'B' Company of the 9th Royal Scots managed to fight its way into the Works and into a German trap. The unwounded survivors of 'A' Company, led by their 22 year old company sergeant major, Jack Renwick M.C., M.M., set off in an apparent attempt to support the remainder of 'B' Company fighting for their lives inside the buildings. the small party was last seen about 11 a.m. disappearing into the smoke and dust. None of the Royal Scots, or their bodies, were ever seen or heard of again.

The third type of engagement which has been omitted is that where the P.B.I. were mown down as they advanced in nice, neat lines before they ever made contact with the enemy. On 1st July 1916, the first day of the Battle of the Somme, the cream of Britain's volunteers in the battalions of Kitchener's New Armies went over the top to be slaughtered. The Official History comments, "The extended lines started in excellent order, but gradually melted away. There was no wavering or attempting to come back, the men fell in their ranks, mostly before the first hundred yards of No-Man's-Land had been crossed." Casualties for the day amounted to 2426 officers and 54,459 rank and file killed, wounded or missing (missing being synonymous with blown to bits), a total of over half the attacking force. Only 12 officers and 573 other ranks were taken prisoner.

Nearly 600 of the (1st Tyneside Scottish) Northumberland Fusiliers, including every officer and sergeant lay dead in No-Man's-Land. The War Diary for the 10th (Service) Battalion, Prince of Wales' Own (West Yorkshire) Regiment records the loss of 22 officers, including the C.O., the second-in-command and the adjutant, and about 750 other ranks. On this disastrous day another 18 of Kitchener's New Army battalions, in addition to seven regular, four Territorial and one Empire (the 1st Newfoundland) suffered losses of over 500 officers and men.

The Newfoundlanders' fate was particularly tragic. They formed part of the reserve brigade of the 29th Division opposite Beaumont Hamel, a German strongpoint, and their brigade was to leap-frog through the first German line once it had been taken. Eight British battalions had already gone over the top in this sector but judging by the numbers of dead and wounded lying in front of the enemy wire it was doubtful how many men, if any, had reached the German position. Rockets had been seen rising from the enemy's first trench but whether these were German or British was not known.

Orders were then passed down from Division through reserve brigade H.Q. to the effect that the 1st Newfoundland battalion was to mount an immediate attack to clear the German front line. The Newfoundlanders' C.O., an Englishman, queried whether their objective was still in German hands and was told that the position was uncertain. In answer to another direct question - was he to move independently of any other reserve unit - the answer was yes. Accordingly, the battalion moved out. The reserve trenches in which they were waiting were some 300 yards behind the British front line and it was a similar distance across No-Man's-Land to the German positions. In view of the urgency of their orders the men went straight over the top from the reserve trenches instead of moving up to the front line through the congested and battered communication trench.

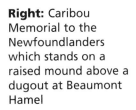

Right: Caribou Memorial to the Newfoundlanders which stands on a raised mound above a dugout at Beaumont Hamel

As soon as the assaulting infantry appeared the German machine-gunners zeroed in on this excellent target and opened fire. There was no covering artillery barrage for the attackers and the enemy, free of the necessity to keep their heads down, were able to give the 752 advancing Newfoundland officers and men their undivided attention. Before they even entered No-Man's Land the infantry were forced to crowd together as they passed through the narrow channels in the several belts of British barbed wire. These gaps constituted a ready made killing zone for the German guns and unwounded Newfound-landers were forced to tread over the bodies of their less fortu-nate comrades. The few dozen men who managed to cross No-Man's-Land were shot down as they desperately tried to find a path through the enemy wire.

Just 40 minutes after the attack started, 26 officers and 658 rank and file, or 91% of the attacking force, had been killed or wounded. The battalion had been destroyed for nothing, and in fact it is doubtful whether the sacrifice of the gallant men from Newfoundland had resulted in the death of even one German soldier.

1
Over by Christmas?
The 1st Royal Warwicks
go to War

Sunday the 23rd August 1914 at 4.30 a.m. and Boulogne quayside echoed the accents of Birmingham and Coventry as the 1st Battalion, Royal Warwickshire Regiment, part of the 10th Infantry Brigade of the newly formed 4th Division, disembarked in France. Laden with kit, tired and indifferently fed, the men were packed into a waiting troop train. The last straggler whose surname had been a boon to N.C.O.s since his recruit days, Private Daft, was hustled aboard by acting Corporal Green and the Warwicks finally steamed off to war.

The old sweats, veterans of the Sudan, South Africa and India, went to sleep or discussed the interesting position of men who were time-expired in the middle of a war. (They were sent home on leave, deemed to have automatically re-enlisted, and then returned to the front to be fed back into the trenches): For Alf Williams from Newcastle and Len Rhodes from Dudley Borough, whose regimental numbers were respectively 3 and 8, this was a matter of some importance. At the other end of the train young soldiers like Billy Weston, who had promised his widowed mother two letters a week, wrote home on note pads or field service cards before settling down. The two Wall brothers, who always seemed uneasy whenever they were apart, sat leaning against each other and dozed.

In their first class carriages the officers reviewed the past and considered the future. The commanding officer, Lieut. Colonel John Elkington, had taken over the battalion some six months previously and might even hope for a brigade if the war lasted long enough. The majors had seen it all before and William Christie, with five medals and three daughters to his credit, had once been the youngest major in the British Army. His companion Ronald Meiklejohn, whom he had known since their school days at Rugby, had already won the D.S.O. in the Boer War. Among the captains, Charles Bentley was the only officer whose service did not conform to the usual pattern. Leaving

Edinburgh University where he was studying his father's profession he had abandoned the medicine bottle for a sword and enlisted as a private in the Royal Scots Greys, with whom he had served throughout the South African War. Finally convincing his family that he wished to be a soldier and not a doctor he was gazetted into the Warwicks in 1902. He had promised his son Charles, age seven, a German pickelhaube. The subalterns, their swords newly sharpened in the armourers shop in accordance with standing orders, had no misgivings. Admittedly the senior subaltern, who had joined the battalion on the North West Frontier of India in 1908, did not quite believe a senior officer's advice that in time of war everything was provided and money was not necessary. He had brought with him £10 in gold, just in case. The most junior, young Denis Deane a newly gazetted Second Lieutenant with just eight days service, was frankly delighted. His father, a retired major, in common with other well informed opinion thought the war might well be over by Christmas. It would be extremely bad luck to miss such an opportunity at the start of his professional career.

For many indeed the war would be over by Christmas. Their colonel would be cashiered and disgraced whilst Major Meiklejohn, wounded in his first action, would spend four years in a prisoner of war camp. The senior subaltern, who in another war was to become Field Marshal Montgomery of Alamein, was much luckier but even so he would spend 72 hours hiding by day and moving by night behind the German cavalry screen. As for the remainder, Major Christie would never again see his daughters, nor Captain Bentley his son, or Deane his father. Corporal Green would not be harassed by Private Daft, the old soldiers would not have to worry about their pensions and the Wall boys would always be together. Billy Weston's mother would receive only one letter - her son's expectation of life was now a matter of hours. For by Christmas they, and many more, would be dead.

At 10.30 a.m. on Monday 24th August the Warwicks hastily detrained at Le Cateau. The Battle of Mons had been fought the previous day and the British Army had already begun to retreat. By 2 a.m. on the 25th, whilst helping to cover the retirement of the 3rd and 5th Infantry Divisions, the 10th Brigade had marched northwards nearly as far as St. Python. Later that day the brigade withdrew to Quievy and then moved south-west during the night to Haucourt. As the result of taking a wrong turning near Caudry the Warwicks appear to have marched further than the rest of their brigade.

By 6 a.m. on Wednesday 26th August, the 568th anniversary of the Battle of Crécy, the 10th Brigade was bivouacked in cornfields near the village of Haucourt. Officers and men alike were dog tired as they watched the heavy mist, prelude to yet another scorching day, begin to lift. A few minutes later the 1st King's Own (Royal Lancaster Regiment) formed up in quarter-column, preparatory to entrenching, on the brow of a hill a few hundred yards north of the Warwicks. Suddenly a number of enemy machine-guns opened at close range followed almost immediately afterwards by the fire of two or three German field gun batteries. Caught in close formation the hapless King's Own lost 12 officers, including their colonel, and 431 men killed, wounded, or missing in the space of ten minutes. At this point

Below: British infantry resting during the retreat from Mons.

the two forward Warwick companies dashed forward to the rescue, although what they hoped to achieve is questionable. There are three different versions of how this counter-attack was launched. According to *Military Operations France and Belgium, 1914* Volume 1, Page 155, the attack was ordered by direction of a staff officer. The regimental history gives a different account and states that the men spontaneously extended and charged forward under Major Christie. It adds that the attack thus made without orders was not 'well-advised.' The third version comes from the pen of Field Marshal Montgomery who records, 'The C.O. galloped up to us... and shouted to us to attack the enemy on the forward hill at once. This was the only order; there was no reconnaissance, no plan, no covering fire.'

On reaching the crest the two Warwicks companies were swept back with heavy losses. Among the dead was 9798 Private Billy Weston and the wounded included seven officers, one of whom was Major Meiklejohn - in a few hours time he would be a prisoner of war. The Warwicks then fell back to positions on the Haucourt-Ligny road where they suffered further casualties from heavy shelling. At 3 p.m. 'A' Company withdrew as escort to the guns. (This was probably the 27th Battery, R.F.A. which succeeded in moving through heavy enemy fire with comparatively few casualties.) Later, at about 6.30 p.m., Lieut. Colonel Elkington with about 60 men retired on Ligny, the next village to the east and the scene of fierce fighting. Why the C.O. should have left the remainder of his battalion is not known. In the event this left Major Poole of the Warwicks with three companies, which included the two badly mauled forward companies plus two companies of the 1st Royal Dublin Fusiliers, still holding the road.

During the evening Haucourt was taken by units of the German 13th Reserve Infantry Brigade supported by extensive artillery fire. By this time the left flank was wide open whilst on the right the 1st Gordon Highlanders had begun a fighting retreat. Most of that battalion, including 14 officers would be overwhelmed and captured early the next morning. Left without orders and in danger of being surrounded Major Poole determined to retire; a painful decision since without transport the wounded would have to be left behind. The actual time of withdrawal varies according to different authorities. The earliest is 7.30 p.m., according to the battalion's war

Opposite page: First phase of the Retreat from Mons.
A. British Positions at Mons.
B. Retiring Line of 2nd Army Corps, August 24.
C. British Lines, evening, August 24.
D. British Lines, August 25–26.
E. Position of General Sordet's Cavalry, August 23–26.
F. General direction of French Retreat.
G. General d'Amande's movement from Arras to assist the British.
H. British Lines, August 26–27.
J. British Lines, August 28

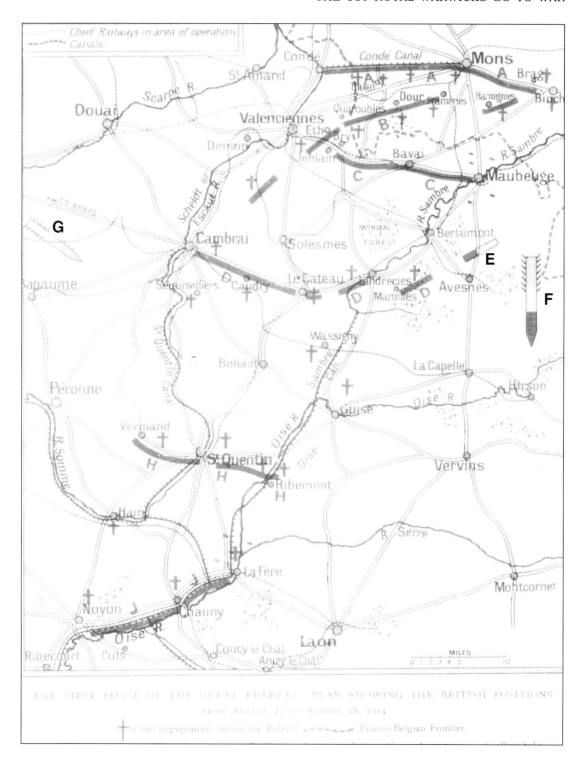

THE FIRST PHASE OF THE GREAT RETREAT. PLAN SHOWING THE BRITISH POSITIONS
FROM AUGUST 23 TO AUGUST 28, 1914.

diary, while the latest is 11 p.m. (*Military Operations 1914*, Volume 1, Page 189); a substantial difference of 3½ hours. Whatever the actual time it is certain that for the next three days Major Poole and his men, together with a future Field Marshal, played a deadly game of hide and seek behind the German advance.

Late the next afternoon, over twenty miles away, the Grande Place of St. Quentin was thronged with British infantrymen, many of them from the 1st battalions of the Warwicks and Dublin Fusiliers. These men had tramped beneath a blazing August sun utterly weary, dispirited, hungry and only sustained by liberal quantities of wine given them by French peasants. Now in the square scores were sleeping on the pavements or propped up against shop fronts whilst others, completely exhausted, lay full-length on the cobbles. According to an eye-witness most of them were not only without arms but had also abandoned their equipment and many, literally, had bellies full of wine and boots half-full of blood. Lieut. Colonel Elkington and the C.O. of the Dublins had asked the mayor for food, medical supplies and permission to rest the men. The mayor, fearing German reprisals or a battle which would destroy his beautiful town refused their requests - unless the two senior officers signed an agreement to surrender. Dazed by lack of sleep and exhausted by the events of the past three days the two colonels put their signatures to a paper which gave the numbers of men and the names of officers who were prepared to capitulate.

This was the situation when Major Tom Bridges of the 4th Dragoon Guards with part of his squadron, together with a few Lancers, horse gunners and other stragglers, reached the town. Appalled by the spectacle in the square, Bridges and his officers began to form the men into some sort of order and meanwhile commandeered every horse and cart in the town and requisitioned supplies of food. All this took time and it was not until after midnight that they were ready to move. Preceded by a makeshift band of tin whistles, Jew's harps and a toy drum, with the wounded and exhausted laid in a motley collection of carts, the column of nearly 500 men lurched and stumbled westwards through the night mist towards Savy. A few minutes later a metallic rattle on the cobbles heralded the approach of German cavalry entering the town through one of the darkened side streets leading into the Grande Place. Elkington had already left the town by himself, but for what purpose or to which destination is not known.

The entry in the battalion's war diary for the next day reads, '28-8-14. Col. Elkington plus 280 men rejoined the Xth Brigade with Major C. Christie.' However subsequent entries are signed by 'A. J. Poole, Major Commanding 1 R Warwicks.' Lieut. Colonel Elkington, together with his brother colonel, damned by his signature on the surrender document was awaiting trial by General Court Martial charged under Part 1, Section 4 of the Army Act. This section, which carried the death penalty dealt with soldiers who shamefully delivered up 'any garrison, place or post or guard' which it was their duty to defend. Fortunately for both the accused the charge against them was reduced to a lesser offence of 'behaving in a scandalous manner unbecoming the character of an officer and a gentleman' in that they, at St. Quentin on 27th August 1914, during a retirement following upon an engagement at Ligny, without due cause, agreed together to surrender themselves and the troops under their respective command. The General Court Martial of the two officers was held on 12th September 1914 and both were found guilty and sentenced to be cashiered. The sentences were confirmed by the Commander-in-Chief and promulgated two days later.

Rested and reinforced the 1st Warwicks moved north into Belgium. On the afternoon of 13th October 1914, in an attack on the semi-fortified village of Meteren dominated by its church steeple, the battalion lost 50 killed and three times that number wounded. Lieut. Montgomery, sniped by a German marksman firing from the steeple, was among the wounded. The dead included privates 3 Williams and 8 Rhodes, Corporal Green, Herbert Daft and the Wall boys, who would stay together in death as they had in life. Two men each earned a Distinguished Conduct Medal dragging the fallen Major Christie behind cover, under very heavy enemy fire, but he died of his wounds within an hour. Both Captain Bentley and 2/Lieut. Deane still had another ten days to live.

Christmas 1914 passed and 157 officers and men had been killed and over 300 wounded. Recruits who had never heard of Alf Williams and newly commissioned officers who had not known Lieut. Colonel Elkington joined the battalion. As the war dragged on through 1915, with the battles of Neuve Chapelle and Ypres and the constant trench warfare, the casualties mounted month by month. Meanwhile, in another part of the Western Front, a fresh chapter was being added to the story of the 1st Warwicks.

28th September 1915 and bugles sounded in a French sector as the 1st Battalion, 2nd Infantry Regiment, of the French Foreign Legion went over the top. Company B 3, which included two Americans and a rather taciturn Englishman, had drawn the position of honour - Navarin Farm. As men dropped like flies Company B 3, or what was left of it, passed the first two lines of wire and slithered into Horseshoe Wood. The trees splintered under the impact of shell blasts and bullets as the men moved slowly forward covering German dugouts and trying to pinpoint enemy machine-gunners. Across one more line of trenches before entering the left-hand edge of the wood and the notorious strongpoint - Navarin Farm. The Englishman was in front of his section, bombing and waving them forward as he had done at Hill 119 at Souchez cemetery in the last big attack, when another hidden machine-gun opened up. His right leg smashed by several bullets he pitched into a rain-filled trench. It was long after nightfall before the stretcher bearers found him.

Above: Lt.-Col. John Ford Elkington D.S.O.

For nearly a year he lay in a Paris hospital recovering from his wounds. Then, in the summer of 1916 as the staff and orderlies stood rigidly to attention, a visiting general stood by the Englishman's bed and read out a citation from the French Official Journal. 'The Medaille Militaire and the Croix de Guerre avec Palme are conferred upon No. 29274 Legionnaire John Ford Elkington of the First Foreign Regiment. Although fifty years old, he has given proof during the campaign of remarkable courage and ardour, setting everyone the best possible example. He was gravely wounded on September 28, 1915, rushing forward to assault enemy trenches. He has lost the use of his right leg.' In October 1914 Elkington had sought the traditional refuge of Englishmen in trouble and travelled to Paris to join the Legion.

The French citation was brought to the notice of King George V and a few weeks later Elkington's name again appeared in the *London Gazette*. 'H.M. the King has been graciously pleased to approve the reinstatement of John Ford Elkington of the Royal Warwickshire Regiment with his previous seniority, in conse-

EX-COLONEL REGAINS HIS LOST RANK.

Officer of Warwickshires Who Made Good by Gallant Deeds.

FOREIGN LEGION ROMANCE

Behind an announcement in the *London Gazette* last night lies a romance, surely quite one of the old-style romances, of the great war.

It is the story of how a former lieutenant-colonel of a famous regiment who lost his rank won it back again in his same regiment by his gallant deeds as a legionnaire in the famous Foreign Legion of France.

The story, of which two chapters only are known, and those in the form of brief official statements, is contained in the *London Gazette* of two dates.

CHAPTER ONE.—TIME, 1914.

October 30, 1914.—The *London Gazette* publishes the following War Office announcement:—

Royal Warwickshire Regiment.—Lieutenant-Colonel John F. Elkington is cashiered by sentence of a general court-martial. Dated September 14, 1914.

CHAPTER TWO.—TIME, 1916.

Last Night.—The following announcement is made in the *London Gazette*:

Royal Warwickshire Regiment.—The The King has been graciously pleased to approve of the reinstatement of John Ford Elkington in the rank of lieutenant-colonel with his previous seniority in consequence of his gallant conduct while serving in the ranks of the Foreign Legion of the French Army.

He is accordingly reappointed lieutenant-colonel in the Royal Warwickshire Regiment, dated August 22, 1916, with seniority from April 6, 1910, and to count service in that rank towards retirement on retired as from February 24, 1914, but without pay or allowances for the period September 14, 1914, to August 21, 1916, inclusive.

The story of the Foreign Legion of France, which was established eighty-five years ago, must be made up of many strange histories and romances, but this episode of this soldier who has won back his right to his rank of lieutenant-colonel in the British Army must be among the brightest stories in its archives.

quence of his gallant conduct while serving in the ranks of the Foreign Legion of the French Army.' On 28th October 1916 Lieut. Colonel Elkington received the insignia of the Distinguished Service Order from the King.

Years passed and finally the war was over by Christmas, but it was to be Christmas 1918 and not 1914. On 10th June 1919 the 1st Royal Warwicks returned to England having spent the entire war on the Western Front - the veterans of Haucourt were few and far between. Major Meiklejohn, repatriated from Germany in April 1918 was serving with the North Russian Expeditionary Force as General Staff Officer 1 (Intelligence). Major Montgomery D.S.O. was preparing to enter the Staff College and Major Poole D.S.O. would one day be the lieut. colonel of the 1st Battalion. At his Berkshire home near Newbury a retired colonel, who never wore his medals, even on Armistice Day, moved awkwardly and only with the aid of a stout walking stick.

Across France and Belgium, as mothers and widows mourned back in England, officers of the Imperial War Graves Commission plotted the positions of markers and graves of nearly 1,500 officers and men of the battalion.

The 1st Royal Warwicks had gone to war.

(Extracts from the war diary of the 1st Battalion, Royal Warwickshire Regiment, Public Record Office W.O.95/1484, are Crown copyright and appear by permission of the Controller of Her Majesty's Stationery Office).

2
'Nothing to Worry About!'
1st Cheshires, Battle of Mons
22nd August 1914

A rearguard action, usually against overwhelming odds, was the fate of many regiments of the B.E.F. including the 1st Battalion Cheshire Regiment, during the first weeks of the war. The Cheshires, at full war strength with 30 officers and 997 other ranks disembarked at Le Havre on Sunday 16th August 1914, detrained at Le Cateau on the 18th, and marched five miles to Pommereuil. The battalion formed part of the 15th Infantry Brigade of the 5th Division, II Corps, and enjoyed a reputation as one of the best shooting and marching formations of the British Army. 9461 Drummer Baker was entrusted with the miniature Colour, a quarter size replica of the Regimental Colour, which had been worked and presented by the ladies of the regiment in 1911. It was competed for each year and awarded to the best shooting Company. The officers agreed that the Colour, flying from its staff 49½ inches long and surmounted by a gilt lion, would be

Below: Old Contemptibles. 1st Cheshires leaving Derry for the Front, 14th August 1914.

borne at the head of the battalion when it marched into Berlin.

At about 3 a.m. on Friday 21st the men were roused and made a forced march 30 miles towards Mons, stopping short at Bossu at noon the next day. After a wearisome stint of digging trenches (later used by the Manchesters) and another forced march along six miles of cobbled roads, the battalion was rushed into a position just north-east of Audregnies. Here, together with the 1st Norfolks, it was to act as a flank guard to the rest of 5th Division retiring on the right.

At this juncture the B.E.F. was facing an enemy greatly superior in numbers and vastly superior in artillery and machine-guns. The British right flank was guarded by a French army with a commander who was liable to retire quite suddenly and without bothering to inform his allies. On the extreme left of the British positions lay the 5th Division and on the extreme left of that Division lay the 1st Cheshires. The task of the Cheshires and Norfolks was to hold their ground until the Division, and with it the rest of the B.E.F., could be withdrawn in some sort of conformity with the movements of the erratic General Lanrezac. Hence every hour gained by the flank guard would be of incalculable value to the main body of British troops.

The Cheshires were allocated a front of over a mile which left them spread very thinly on the ground. Captain Shore with half of 'B' Company took up a position on the northern edge of Audregnies, on the extreme left of the Cheshires' line, while the rest of the company under Capt. Jolliffe was on the left of a deserted cottage on the main Audregnies road. The battalion's two machine-guns, commanded by Lieut. Randall, were sited one on each side of this cottage. Capt. Dyer's 'A' Company occupied a front of some 200 yards extending right from the cottage. 'C' Company, Capt. Dugmore, and 'D' Company under Captains Jones and Rich, extended the line to the right of 'A' Company. Captain Jackson and Lieut. Frost with 'G' Company plus battalion H.Q. were on the roadway. By 7 o'clock that evening five of the officers, including Jones and Frost, would be dead and another fourteen wounded and prisoners of war. The C.O., Jolliffe, Randall, Dyer and Dugmore would be among the latter.

There were considerable gaps between the companies who were unable to see each other owing to the undulating ground, although each company placed a firing line in the cornfields to their front. In addition, the Cheshires were not given the opportunity to entrench or even make a quick reconnaissance of the

Above: The officers, 1st Bn. Cheshire Regiment at Londonderry, 1914.
Back row: Lieut. G. L. F. Houstoun, Lieut. J. C. Sproule, Lieut. T. L. Frost*, 2nd Lieut. Milner.
2nd row from back: Lieut. C. A. K. Matterson, Lieut. H. C. Campbell*, Lieut. H. C. Randall.
Intermediate row: Capt. E. A. Jackson, Capt C. E. Jolliffe, Lieut. H. I. St. J. Hartford*, Lieut. W. G. R. Elliot, Capt V. R. Tahourdin (Adjutant), Capt. J. L. Shore, Capt. B. E. Massey.
Front row: Capt. W. L. E. R. Dugmore, Major D. C. Boger (taking over command), Lieut-Col. H. F. Kellie (handing over command), Capt. A. J. L. Dyer, Capt. E. R. Jones*.

Of the officers appearing in the group, 16 were with the 1st Battalion when it went to the Great War. The four marked * were killed in action. Of the remainder, seven were wounded and four invalided from war service.

ground which they had been ordered to hold at all costs. However, no doubt the C.O., Lieut. Colonel Boger, was heartened when the colonel of the 1st Norfolks (on his right) told him there was a British cavalry screen between them and the enemy and there was 'nothing to worry about.'

At this point both battalions were heavily shelled and enemy infantry could be seen moving from the wood just south of Quievrain and from the northern part of the Bois du Deduit. Almost immediately one of the Cheshires' machine-guns suffered a direct hit and it would appear that two German aeroplanes hovering overhead were spotting for their gunners. The shell fire now began to cause casualties among the men lying in the open and the Cheshire C.O. requested close artillery support. Accordingly, at about 12 noon amid shouts of 'Way for the guns' a section of the 119th Battery, Royal Field Artillery, galloped up the road in fine style with the horses at full stretch. As the gunners reached the rear of 'D' Company's transport they were smothered by a storm of enemy shrapnel and in a matter of seconds the roadway was a mass of struggling horses, men and gun limbers, all piled on top of each other. In the midst of this carnage, and terrified by the screams of injured horses, 'D' Company's ammunition mules stampeded and with other loose transport and gun team animals dashed away down the sloping road.

Meanwhile the 9th Lancers and the 4th Dragoon Guards were just north of Audregnies and in fact two dismounted lancer squadrons were already in action with rifles and Maxims against German infantry trying to infiltrate from the left flank. The terrain was a maze of slag heaps, fields, scattered buildings, sunken roads and railway lines, dominated by the tall chimney of a sugar beet processing factory near the old Roman road. Just after noon two troops of dragoons and two lancer squadrons were ordered to drive back the advancing Germans and relieve the pressure on the flankguard. 'A' and 'C' squadrons of the 9th Lancers followed by the 4th Dragoon Guards came onto the road to the left of the remaining British machine-gun and galloped across the corn field intending to take the enemy in the flank. The horsemen were within 500 yards of their objective when they were checked by wire entanglements which divided two fields of corn. Assailed by every field gun, Maxim and rifle which the enemy could bring to bear the charge disintegrated. When the survivors straggled back to Wargnies-le-Petit that evening only 80 out of 500 men answered the roll, and 200 horses were missing. Admittedly there were still scattered troops and sections which had managed to reach the cover of the sugar factory, cottages or slag heaps, and these were to keep the Germans at bay with rifle fire for nearly four hours.

By 2.30 p.m. three separate runners had been sent by brigade to the Cheshires with orders for them to fall back, but all three messengers had been killed or captured and the order to retire was never received. Thus at 3 p.m. when the Germans launched a massive infantry attack from the Bois du Deduit and began to close with the Cheshires, Colonel Boger looked beyond his right flank and discovered the enemy in a position previously occupied by the Norfolks. The men of Cheshire were now

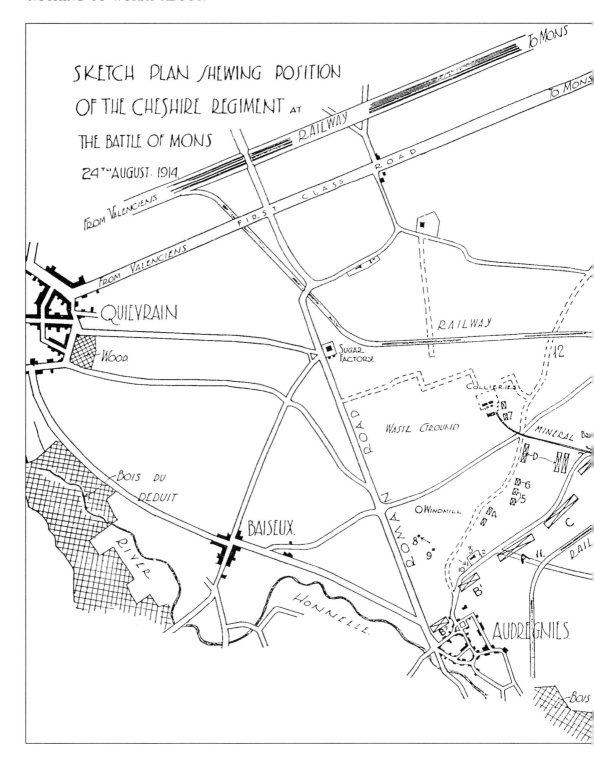

SKETCH PLAN SHEWING POSITION OF THE CHESHIRE REGIMENT AT THE BATTLE OF MONS 24TH AUGUST. 1914.

facing an entire German division and fought a series of fragmented engagements as independent companies or isolated groups.

At about 5.30 p.m. a 'forlorn hope' consisting of 30 men from 'A' Company and the right half of 'B' Company fixed bayonets and led by Captains Dyer, Jolliffe and Massey with drawn swords, plus Lieut. Matterson, charged the enemy with the intention of covering the retirement of the rest of the battalion. This near suicidal attack actually drove back the Germans upon their supports although all three captains were wounded and brought down. In the meantime Capt. Shore had been told by a staff officer to retire to the rear of Audregnies 'where we are going to rally.'

However, Shore and the survivors of his half company were unable to find any rallying point or indeed any troops, apart from a few wounded of the 4th D.G. In any case the village was being so heavily shelled that the men were obliged to keep marching and eventually met up with the main body of Norfolks who had received the order to retire.

Although the order was passed down the line to the men still fighting to break out, or every man for himself, small parties continued the fight until 7 p.m. when, in the words of the *Official History of the War in France and Belgium*, Vol. I, Page 105, '...surrounded and overwhelmed on all sides, they laid down their arms. Of the main body on the Audregnies road, only forty remained unwounded.' The Cheshires had lost 22 officers and 814 other ranks killed, captured or wounded.

Their captors, mostly from the 72nd Infantry Regiment, spent a long time questioning the prisoners as to the whereabouts of

Left: A. 'A' Coy Capt. Dyer. **B1.** Half 'B' Coy Capt. Jolliffe. **B2.** Half 'B' Coy Capt. Shore. **C.** 'C' Coy Capt. Dugmore. **1 & 2.** Machine-guns. **3.** Deserted cottage. **4.** Two platoons of 'A' Coy advanced 150yds from road firing line. **5.** Two platoons of 'C' coy under Capt. Jackson advanced 300yds from road. **6.** One platoon of 'C' Coy afterwards taken up by Capt. Dugmore from road to reduce the gap between his firing line and 'D' coy. **7.** Two platoons of 'D' Coy under Capt. Rich placed in a cart track on either side of a factory at the mineral railway. **1-8.** Bayonet charge by Capt. Dyer's party. Germans had advanced as far as 8. **9.** Capt. Jolliffe wounded in the shoulder on his return for more men to sustain the charge. **10.** Capt. Jolliffe's leg shattered in two places just before reaching his reserves on the road for more men. **11.** Place where Lieut. Campbell was killed. **12.** Coal mines occupied by half company Norfolk Regt. **13.** Position of last stand of a small detachment of Cheshires and Norfolks prior to retirement to St. Waast.

the battalion's many machine-guns. They could not believe that the volume of accurate and damaging fire from the British had been delivered only by riflemen. Before the final surrender Drummer Baker hid the miniature Colour under the eaves of a house in Audregnies from whence it was taken, via a choir stall in the local church, to a girls' school where it was bricked up in a wall. After the Germans received an anonymous letter informing them that a British Colour had been hidden in the village they spent five days searching every house and building. When it could not be found they offered a reward of 2,000 marks (about £100, a substantial sum of money in those days) for its surrender. There were no takers and the Colour was eventually recovered by the Cheshires on 17th November 1918, a week after the Armistice.

Not all the Cheshires were swept up by the Germans. Sergeant Meachin who had been wounded earlier in the afternoon made his way to Brussels where he was sheltered and given false identity papers by nurse Edith Cavell. Disguised as a fish hawker he was successful in reaching Holland and from Flushing managed to reach Folkestone. Private Woods was another evader. He hid in a cornfield until it was dark and then crawled about half a mile to Witheries. There he managed to contact the friendly owner of an estaminet who gave him civilian clothes and hid him for a while in the village. Woods eventually found his way to England and reported to the regimental depot at Chester on 5th March 1915!

Reinforced by drafts of over 500 officers and men, the 1st Battalion again suffered heavily during the Battle of La Bassée. Finally, on 22nd October 1914 the 382 survivors were holding the village of Violaines, just north of La Bassée, when they were swamped by no less than three full battalions of the German VII Corps which attacked at first light. Only 153 officers and men of the Cheshires, many of them wounded, managed to fight their way through the German ring. All but three of the officers who had landed in France two months previously were now either dead, wounded or prisoners of war. The latest casualties included Captain Shore, wounded and a prisoner, and Captain Rich who died of his wounds on 9th November 1914.

After the war, in 1919, some of the Cheshires, in common with men of other regiments, were to benefit from the provisions of Army Order 193 published on 5th May that year. This Order was headed 'Rewards for Officers and Soldiers for services in the field, and for services rendered in captivity or in attempting to escape or in escaping therefrom.' The first paragraph dealt with gallantry in the field, which had to be unconnected with capture rendered prior to 15th November 1917, and substantiated by two first hand witnesses one of whom had to be an officer.

Paragraph 4 in the Order covered, (a) exceptional services rendered by officers and soldiers whilst prisoners of war or interned and, (b) exceptionally gallant conduct and/or determination displayed by officers and soldiers in escaping or attempting to escape from captivity. An additional proviso required that 'no blame has been attached to the individual in respect of original capture.' The 'exceptional services' mentioned in 4(a) ranged from nursing fellow P.O.W.s who were suffering from typhus and were without adequate medical staff or facilities to making a thorough nuisance of oneself to the camp guards and administration.

As a general rule, a successful officer escaper qualified for the Military Cross (a D.S.O. in the case of field officers) or a D.C.M. or M.M. for other ranks. Unsuccessful attempts to escape, however dangerous for the individual, usually earned nothing higher than a mention in despatches. For example, Lieutenant W. G. Morris of the 1st East Surreys, wounded and taken prisoner at the Battle of Mons, made several determined attempts to escape from captivity until, on the last occasion at Schwarnstadt in Hanover on 27th June 1917, he was shot and killed by the German camp guards. He was awarded a posthumous mention under Army Order 193. Very occasionally a man's name was brought to notice under two different headings. Thus, Lieut. Matterson of the 1st Cheshires received a mention for gallantry in the field (at Mons) and a second mention for attempting to escape from his prisoner of war camp.

The record for escape bids appears to be held by Lieut. Jocelyn Hardy of the 2nd Connaught Rangers who finally, and successfully, escaped at his ninth attempt! He rejoined his regiment on the Western Front in 1918 and earned a Military Cross (gazetted 15th October 1918) before losing a foot. Under A.O.193 he was awarded a D.S.O. for gallantry in the field during the retreat from Mons (where he was wounded and taken prisoner) and a bar to his M.C. for his escape from captivity.

In addition to Lieut. Matterson, the following awards were made to the 1st Battalion Cheshire officers and men. The ranks shown are those held in 1919:-

For gallantry in the field (Mons):

D.S.O.

Lt. Col. Boger and Major Shore.

M.C.

Major Dyer and Captain Jolliffe.

D.C.M.

4281 R.S.M. Howard, 4277 Sgt. Raynor and 8261 Private Woodier. Woodier escaped from Osnabruck POW camp on his second attempt on 7th April 1918 and crossed the Dutch frontier a week later. Apparently he was not decorated for his successful escape.

M.M.

8013 Sgt. Barrow (M.G. section) and 8799 Sgt. Smith.

M.I.D.

Capt. Randall, 6893 Pte. Moore, 7963 Pte. Spencer and 9327 Pte. Taylor - these last two manned the surviving machine-gun.

For escaping or attempting to escape:

M.M.

Privates 7234 Farmer, 7611 Harrison, 9999 Lavin and 8726 Southern.

M.I.D.

Capt. Elliott and 7518 L/Cpl. Lewis. There were also three awards for the action at La Bassée and seven M.S.M.s to other ranks for valuable services whilst P.O.W.

3

'Fix Bayonets!'

2nd King's Own Yorkshire Light Infantry, Battle of Le Cateau 26th August 1914

When the 2nd Battalion, The King's Own (Yorkshire Light Infantry) mobilised for war there was only one slight hitch - six sets of heavy draught horse harness had gone astray! This deficiency was made good by courtesy of Guinness' Brewery in Dublin and the battalion duly sailed from Ireland, where they had been stationed, for France. The Yorkshiremen, together with the 2nd King's Own Scottish Borderers, 2nd Duke of Wellington's (West Riding Regiment) and the 1st Queen's Own (Royal West Kent Regiment) formed the 13th Infantry Brigade, 5th Division, II Corps which finally moved into Belgium at 9 a.m. on 22nd August 1914. As the KOYLI 1st battalion was still soldiering in Singapore the officers and men of the 2nd blessed their good fortune in being the first of their regiment into action, especially as it would probably be a short war. It would be even shorter for 2/Lieutenant Pepys, the battalion's young machine-gun officer, his life expectancy could now be measured in hours.

Below: 2/Lt. John Pepys.

The 13th Infantry Brigade was ordered to hold the line of the Mons-Condé Canal, from Les Herbières to Marietta, a frontage of three miles. The two forward battalions were the West Kents on the right with the Borderers on the left, supported respectively by the West Ridings and the Yorkshiremen with the KOYLI machine-gun detachment to the front between the two leading units. At about 1 p.m. on Sunday 23rd after the British positions had been heavily shelled enemy formations attacked along the entire front. The two KOYLI machine-gun crews held their fire until massed German infantry attempted to storm the St. Ghislain bridge which spanned the canal. This attack was made by the Brandenberg Grenadier Regiment whose losses were so

Left: Le Cateau: awaiting the German attack.

heavy that, according to a German account, the regiment was practically destroyed. As the enemy troops fell back 2/Lieut. John Pepys was killed by a sniper firing from a tree on the opposite bank. The family's other son, 2/Lieut. Francis Pepys, would be killed in action on 14th November 1914.

After their part in the Battle of Mons the KOYLI, together with the remainder of the Corps, fell back until by mid-afternoon on the 25th the battalion reached Le Cateau. The men were fed and settled down for the night with 'A' Company on outpost duty, but at 2.35 a.m. on the 26th orders came for a further retirement and the news that the Borderers and KOYLI were to act as rearguard for the Division. It was calculated that the divisional transport would not be clear before 11 a.m. and the rearguard troops were to hold their positions until that hour, when they could make a fighting withdrawal. It was still dark when the battalion moved forward to find its allotted front, which stretched north and south of the Bavai-Reumont road. However, the situation was complicated by the arrival of the 122nd and 123rd Field Batteries R.A., which took post within the line of infantry supports and with their teams and limbers packed in a sunken road which ran diagonally from Le Cateau to Troisvilles. This effectively severed communication between the various parts of the KOYLI battalion. The KOYLI machine-guns were now commanded by Lieut. de Unett, and L/Cpl. King and Pte. Mitchell distinguished themselves by digging pits for the guns while under heavy shrapnel fire. At 6 a.m. the following message from Brigade H.Q. was passed to the C.O., 'O.C. 2/KOYLI - Orders have been changed. There will be NO retirement for the fighting troops; fill up your trenches with water, food and ammunition.'

Le Cateau had been in German hands since the small hours and this gave the enemy command of all the dead ground as well as commanding positions for his artillery. The storm burst at 8 a.m. when the British line was swept by high explosive and shrapnel shells. 'D' Company posted near the cross roads held off the first infantry frontal attacks and also managed to bring diagonal fire to bear on the enemy who had reached the top of the cutting through which ran the road to Cambrai. The remainder of the battalion was heavily engaged along its front and also, shortly after 11 a.m., some of the KOYLI trenches were enfiladed from rising ground on the south side of the Cambrai road. About 12.45 p.m. an order was passed to retire any field gun that could be moved from the central sector. However, the movement of what was left of the gun teams triggered a deluge of German shells and only two guns could be brought out; the rest remained silent on the ground with their dead crews lying around them. One of the two guns was extricated by a KOYLI, 9376 L/Cpl. F.W. Holmes who had already brought himself to notice by carrying a wounded comrade on his back out of the firing line under what his V.C. citation described as 'desperate

Right: Le Cateau 26th August 1914.

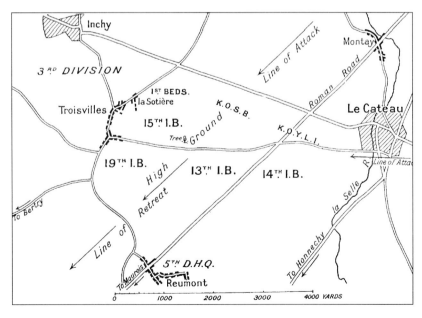

33

circumstances.' Holmes then ran to one of the gun teams which was limbered up with its gun, but with all the detachment killed, and succeeded in bringing it out of the battle, at first with the aid of a trumpeter, who was then killed, and finally single-handed.

Following a softening-up bombardment, two enemy battalions in close formation advanced over the ridge near Le Cateau to within 600 yards of 'B' Company. The defenders held their fire until the approaching mass was well down the forward slope and then opened rapid fire with rifles and the remaining machine-gun. After some initial confusion the Germans rolled back over the ridge leaving the ground strewn with dead and wounded. Meanwhile 'D' Company was in difficulties having suffered heavy casualties plus the fact that the forward platoons were running out of ammunition. Captain L. Simpson led a reinforcement from the supports toward the trenches under heavy fire but he was wounded on the way. The men were rallied by 6923 Sergeant Archibald MacDonald who had already won the D.C.M. in South Africa in 1899, when serving with the Hampshire Regiment, and was to be awarded the French Medaille Militaire for his overall gallantry in action between the 21st and 30th August 1914. At about 1.30 p.m. further to the left, Lieut. Butt with half of No.11 Platoon of 'C' Company, reinforced the firing line and Sergt. A. W. Patterson (whose commission was dated from that day) brought up the second half of the platoon. They continued to occupy their trenches until badly enfiladed from higher ground to the north, but at about 3.30 p.m., finding the position untenable, they attempted to retire. Lieut. Butt was wounded and Sgt. Patterson would never dine in the officers mess; he was killed outright.

Meanwhile at 3.25 p.m. Captain Luther tried to reinforce the 'A' Company trenches held by Capt. Gatacre. He was accompanied by 2/Lieuts. Slingsby and Ritchie with their respective platoons, but the intervening ground was swept by hostile fire and only a dozen men reached their objective. Capt. Luther was wounded in the attempt and 2/Lieut. Ritchie killed. Lieut. Denison (who had started his service career as a midshipman in the Royal Navy) was holding a section of the trench at this point when he was blinded by a rifle bullet through the temple. His men bandaged him and propped him up against the side of the trench, from when he continued to cheer and encourage them. He was unconscious by the end of the day and died some weeks later in hospital at Mons, a prisoner in German hands.

Elsewhere on the battlefield the divisional trains had made good their escape and at about 3 p.m. the brigade reserve battalion was observed retiring to the rear covering the withdrawal of other troops. However, there was no question of retreat for the men in the firing line, even had such an order been received, owing to the proximity of the enemy and the nature of the ground. Some of the men in the lines of support however, did receive a direct order from Brigade H.Q. to fall back and thus a portion of the battalion was saved. Some of the trenches were now without ammunition, the remaining machine-gun was smashed, and in the closing stages of the fight some officers told their men they could take their chance of breaking out. Ten men of 'B' Company, led by 5216 Sgt. Richards, were among the few who successfully evaded the closing ring of Germans. Sgt. Richards, one of the battalion's old soldiers, had nearly completed 18 years service and was looking forward to receiving his long service and good conduct medal.

For the last hour of the fight, so far as they could see, the KOYLI alone were facing the German advance. Although Germans surrounded the battalion on three sides and were supported by field guns brought up within 900 yards of the trenches, the enemy still hesitated to make the final advance. Time and again their bugles sounded the British Army 'Cease Fire' and attempts were made to parley under a flag of truce but each overture was answered with bursts of fire - from those who still had ammunition. Eventually the left companies' positions were overrun and German infantry rushed the trenches from four points of the compass. Major Yate gave the order, 'Fix bayonets' to the survivors of his company and led them against a mass of Germans. Yate fell badly wounded and his sergeant, 8840 J. W. Clark, who would also have been a commissioned officer this day, was killed. There was no surrender, as such, for the survivors were mobbed and swamped by a rising tide of grey-coated enemy infantry.

Losses of the battalion at Le Cateau totalled 600, made up of 18 officers, 21 sergeants, 22 corporals and 539 privates. Out of this number 290 were killed and 310, of whom 170 were wounded, taken prisoner.

Major Charles Yate had a colourful military career which started with operations on the North-West Frontier of India in 1897/8 with the Tirah Expeditionary Force and then in the South Africa War 1899/1902 where he was dangerously

wounded and mentioned in despatches. He was attached
to the Japanese Army in Manchuria as an observer
during the Russo-Japanese War 1904/5 and received
the Order of the Sacred Treasure, 4th class, and the
Japanese War Medal. For his bravery at Le Cateau
he was awarded the Victoria Cross. His citation in
the *London Gazette* on 25th November 1914 reads,
'Commanded one of the two companies that
remained to the end in the trenches at Le Cateau
on the 26th August, and when all other officers
were killed or wounded and ammunition exhausted
led his nineteen survivors against the enemy in a
charge in which he was severely wounded. He was
picked up by the enemy and subsequently died as a
prisoner of war.' This last sentence disguises the fact that
he was killed while attempting to escape from a prisoner of
war camp near Torgau, Saxony, on 20th September 1914, with
his wounds barely healed. One source stated that he was shot
by a German guard but another authority writes that he was
found in mysterious circumstances with his skull battered in
(by a German rifle butt?).

Above: Major Charles
Allix Lavington Yate
V.C.

The gallant Sergeant MacDonald was awarded a clasp to his
D.C.M for conspicuous gallantry at Illies on 19th October 1914,
but by the time it was gazetted on 17th December 1914 he was
already dead; killed by a sniper's bullet on 28th October.
Sergeant Richards' entitlement to his long service and good
conduct medal was promulgated in Army Order 412, published
in October 1914, but Richards never lived to wear his long
awaited medal - he was killed in action on 30th October.

After the war the following awards were made to the battalion
under Army Order 193:

For gallantry in the field:

M.C.

Captains Ackroyd, Luther and Lancelot Simpson.

D.C.M.

6556 C.Q.M.S. Gregg, 7214 Sgt. Mullins and 8280 Lance/Sgt.
Sleigh.

M.M.

Privates 8570 Alford, 6130 Mitchell, 8558 Scott and 9047
Usher.

M.I.D.

Major de Unett and 7061 Sgt. Booth.

For valuable services whilst a prisoner:

M.S.M.

8276 Sgt. Boyce and 9043 Pte. Davis.

The Yorkshiremen (although Booth was a Scot) were still full of fight even as prisoners and no less than five members of the battalion received the M.M. for escaping or attempting to escape from captivity:

7061 C.S.M. Booth, 9475 Pte. Child, 8001 Pte. Huggett, 7744 Pte Stones and 27955 Pte. Littlewood.

Right: Facsimile letter from King George V sent to all returning British prisoners of war. Shown smaller than actual size of 240mm x 180mm approximately.

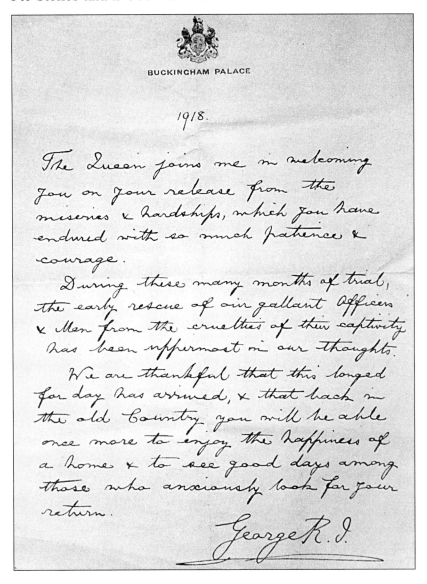

BUCKINGHAM PALACE

1918.

The Queen joins me in welcoming you on your release from the miseries & hardships, which you have endured with so much patience & courage.

During these many months of trial, the early rescue of our gallant Officers & Men from the cruelties of their captivity has been uppermost in our thoughts.

We are thankful that this longed for day has arrived, & that back in the old Country you will be able once more to enjoy the happiness of a home & to see good days among those who anxiously look for your return.

George R.I.

4

'You are Going to Fight it out Here'
2nd Suffolks, Le Cateau, 26th August 1914

Another unit which was swamped whilst acting as rearguard to the 5th Division was the 2nd Battalion, Suffolk Regiment. The Suffolks, who were to form part of the 14th Infantry Brigade of the original B.E.F., began to move from the Curragh in Ireland when war was declared and disembarked at Le Havre on 17th August 1914. Next evening the battalion detrained at Le Cateau and marched on to Landrecies, a distance of about eight miles. Here the men rested until the afternoon of the 20th when orders were received to advance northwards into Belgium, and on the following morning the entire Division moved off along the western edge of the Mormal forest. The 14th Brigade was the centre column of three which marched to Bavai with the men in high spirits despite a hot and dusty journey of seventeen miles.

Unfortunately, there was practically no information available as to the location of their French allies, none at all on the whereabouts of the Germans, and precious little as to the movement of the other British divisions. On the night of 21/22nd August the Suffolks were billeted in St. Waast where, early that evening, a French cavalry patrol passed through on its way to Lille. This was the first that the battalion had seen of the French Army at the Front.

By Sunday August 23rd the 2nd were about nine miles west of Mons and about one mile south of the Mons-Condé canal. Meanwhile, the Germans in great strength were advancing rapidly and because of their enormous weight of artillery were able to drive a wedge between the 3rd and 5th Divisions. As soon as it was dark the British troops were ordered to fall back and this retirement was the start of the strategic movement which history later recorded as the Retreat from Mons. The 5th Division retreated, almost on the line of the forward route reversed, and at about 10 p.m. on the 25th the Suffolks reached Pont des Quatre Vaux, at a crossroads about half a mile to the west of Le Cateau.

Below: Lt. Edward Geoffrey Myddleton.

Bottom: Lt.-Col. Charles Arthur Hugh Brett D.S.O.

At 3.30 a.m. on 26th August the 5th Division stood to arms. It was then in touch with the 3rd Division on its left but there was no sign of I Corps on their right. Shortly after 4 o'clock that morning the C.O. of the Suffolks, Lieut. Colonel Brett, was informed by a staff officer that the retirement of the British Army would continue and the 14th Infantry Brigade would act as part of the rearguard to the 5th Division and, as far as the Suffolks were concerned, 'You are going to fight it out here.' The official history of the war states, 'The Suffolks in particular, who lay immediately to the west of Le Cateau, were badly placed for a general action: there was much dead ground on every side; the field of fire was for the most part limited and could nowhere be called good; and small valleys and sunken roads at sundry points gave hostile infantry every opportunity of concealing their approach. The battalion, in common with the other troops of the 5th Division, made shift to throw up such entrenchments as it could with its "grubbers" no better tools being available.' The C.O. outlined matters to his company commanders, explaining that he had nothing to do with the position selected and everyone must do the best he could. He impressed upon them that there was to be no retreat.

About 6 a.m. No.15 Platoon of 'D' Company, in a forward position opened fire as enemy patrols and scouts began to appear. The corn stooks had barely been flattened to afford a better field fire, and elementary trenches scratched out, when German artillery began shelling the British position. The second shell landed in the middle of No.15 Platoon killing 2/Lieut. Myddleton and the platoon sergeant, Molineaux, and the company commander, Major Peebles, finding his men enfiladed withdrew them back to the main position. About this time Lieut. Colonel Brett, a veteran of the South African War in which he had won the D.S.O., was mortally wounded and Major Doughty succeeded to the command. The gunners of No.11 Battery, R.F.A. who were in close support behind the Suffolks now became the target for German skirmishers who had crept up onto the knoll of the Montay spur. 'Upon these,' records the official history, 'and also upon a concealed German machine-gun on the Cambrai road the left company of the Suffolks opened fire; but there was some doubt as to the situation, for it never occurred to any of the officers that the high ground immediately to the east and west of Le Cateau would be left open to free occupation by the enemy.'

It was not until 10 a.m. that the enemy infantry appeared in force and in spite of their losses from rapid individual rifle and machine-gun fire they advanced steadily for some time, but were eventually forced to go to ground. Sgt. Spriggs, the machine-gun sergeant, was subsequently awarded the D.C.M. for his behaviour on this occasion. By this time hostile artillery fire of tremendous weight was pounding the Suffolks' position and German planes circled overhead dropping smoke bombs of various colours apparently acting as spotters for the guns. The Suffolks, who were on the extreme right of the British line were now in the process of being enfiladed by enemy infantry. Earlier in the day the Germans had succeeded in manhandling a number of machine-guns into a cutting on the Le Cateau-Cambrai road, immediately in front of the Suffolks and by 11 a.m. the fire from these guns had increased to such an extent that the battalion's position was almost untenable. Before noon two heroic attempts were made by the 2nd Manchesters and the 2nd Argyle and Sutherland Highlanders to reinforce the rearguard but only a few men of these two battalions managed to reach the Suffolk line. In addition the Suffolks' machine-guns were now rapidly running out of ammunition and in attempting to bring up some bandoliers Major Doughty, the acting C.O., was severely wounded in three places. Almost at the same time the adjutant was shot in the head.

According to the official history, 'The Suffolks and Yorkshire Light Infantry, the front line of the 14th and 13th Infantry Brigades, were also assailed by an unceasing storm of shrapnel and high explosive shells... The last gun of the 11th Battery was silenced and the Suffolks, together with their reinforcement of Highlanders, were in a worse plight than ever. Nevertheless, after nearly six hours of incessant and overwhelming fire the right of the British line, which rested on Le Cateau, still held firm.'

By this time the Germans had worked so far round the British right flank that Lieuts. George and Burnand were obliged to turn their men about, facing and firing towards their original rear. To quote the official history yet again, 'Between 2.30 and 2.45 the end came. The Germans had by this time accumulated an overwhelming force in the shelter of the Cambrai road, and they now fell upon the Suffolks from the front, right flank, and right rear. The turning movement, however, did not at once make itself felt, and the Suffolks and Argyles opened rapid fire to their front with terrific effect, two officers of the Highlanders in particular bringing down man after man and counting their scores aloud as at a competition. The Germans kept sounding the British "Cease Fire" and gesticulating to persuade the men to surrender, but in vain. At length a rush of enemy from the rear bore down all resistance and the Suffolks and their Highland comrades were overwhelmed. They had for nine hours been under incessant bombardment which had pitted the whole of the ground with craters, and they had fought to the very last, covering themselves with undying glory.'

According to the regimental history, casualties in the 2nd Battalion, killed, wounded and missing amounted to about 720 all ranks. Of the 25 officers, excluding the quartermaster and medical officer, who had landed in France nine days previously, four were dead and eighteen taken as prisoners of war, of whom ten were wounded, six very seriously. By a quirk of fate one of the German regiments opposed to the 2nd Suffolks at Le Cateau bore the distinction 'Gibraltar' on their badges. This was none other than Hardenberg's Regiment which served with the 12th Foot (later the Suffolk Regiment) in the siege of Gibraltar. In addition, both these regiments and the lineal ancestor of No.11 Field Battery had served together at the Battle of Minden in 1759. Presumably this information, if available, would have been of very faint academic interest to the weary, hungry and deafened survivors of the Suffolks.

Twelve years later, on 29th May 1926, the British II Corps Memorial was unveiled at Le Cateau. The memorial, in the form of a cenotaph stands to the south-west of the town, on the extreme right of the position occupied by the rearguard in the stand made against von Kluck's army. The names of those of the 2nd Suffolks who fell in the battle are inscribed on the north face of the monument.

The following awards under Army Order 193 were made to officers and men of the battalion taken at Le Cateau:
For gallantry in the field:

D.S.O.
Major Doughty and Lieut. Colonel Peebles. Both men were also mentioned in despatches.
M.C.
Captains Cutbill and Theodore George.
D.C.M.
Sergeants 9233 Hooper and 6881 Spriggs.
M.M.
5781 Sgt. Argent.
M.I.D.
Captain Carthew, 4125 C.S.M. Carter, 7691 Sgt. Laws, Lance Corporals 7015 Fayers and 8717 Rumbelow
For valuable services whilst a prisoner:
M.S.M.
4450 C.S.M. Read.
M.I.D.
4426 C.S.M. Crack and 3706 Pte. Goddard.
For escaping from captivity:
M.C.
Captain W. MacLeod Campbell. Escaped after three years in German P.O.W. camp and reached England. In April 1918 took over as C.O. of the 5th Suffolks in Palestine where he was later awarded the D.S.O.
M.M.
41727 Pte. Waller.

Left: The unveiling of the Le Cateau Memorial by General Sir Horace Smith-Dorrien in 1926.

5
Rearguard Action at Etreux
2nd Munsters, Retreat from Mons, 27th August 1914

The only regiment of the British Army to qualify for its own map in the many volumes that comprise the Official History of the War in France and Belgium is the 2nd Battalion Royal Munster Fusiliers (Volume 1, Map No. 12 'The Fights at Fesmy and Etreux'). During the Retreat from Mons the 2nd Munsters occupied the post of honour as rearguard to the 1st (Guards) Brigade which, in turn, acted as rearguard for the 1st Division commanded by Major General Lomax.

On the morning of Thursday 27th August 1914 the Irishmen, supported by two 18-pounders of the 118th Battery, Royal Field Artillery and a troop of the 15th (The King's) Hussars, held the villages of Fesmy and Bergues together with two important road junctions in that immediate area. Approaching them, in a 90° arc from north to east, was an entire German Army Corps preceded by masses of cavalry and backed by an impressive array of artillery. Early in the afternoon, having inflicted savage casualties on twelve battalions of the German 2nd Guards Reserve Division which had attacked Fesmy, the Munsters began to withdraw to the south, disengaging by companies.

At about 5.30 p.m. the battalion reformed outside the village of Oisy, about 1½ miles south-west of Fesmy, and

Below: The action at Etreux.

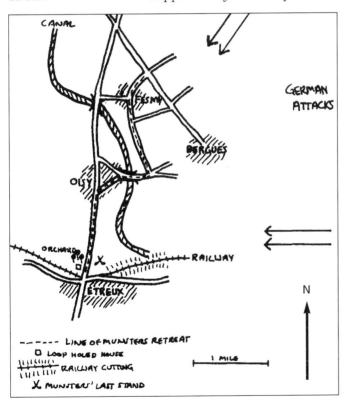

chased off a German dragoon regiment which ominously had appeared from the south. During this action Lieut. Awdry was shot through the lungs and died, sword in hand, at the head of 'E' Company. The rearguard, 'C' Company commanded by Lieut. Deane-Drake with his senior surviving N.C.O., Sergeant T. Foley as 2 i/c, held the village against repeated infantry attacks until the approach bridge spanning a steep-sided canal was effectively blocked with dead and dying Germans. Meanwhile General von Barfeldt, alerted by his punished cavalry from Oisy, altered the line of march of his 19th Infantry Division and moved due west towards Etreux two miles south of the Oisy cross roads.

Moving steadily south the Munsters now tramped along the shallow ditches on both sides of the Oisy-Etreux high road while their two machine-guns, positioned on the actual roadway, fired due north at the badly mauled but numerically very superior German forces. As 'B' Company, the advance guard, approached Etreux they came under heavy rifle and machine-gun fire from houses on the northern outskirts; followed by salvoes from eight German field guns positioned south-east of the village. One of the first shells burst upon the leading 18-pounder gun team, killing or wounding most of the horses and crew and disabling the gun. Now, for the first time, the Irish began to fall fast and although the remaining 18-pounder was brought promptly into action over 300 rounds had already been fired that day and the ammunition was nearly exhausted. Major Charrier, the Munsters C.O. supported by his adjutant Captain Wise, led 'A' and 'B' Companies forward in a desperate bayonet charge; but the Germans had installed themselves in trenches (dug that morning by the Black Watch) and also occupied and loopholed a house west of the road.

Despite heavy casualties, including Major Charrier wounded and down, the Irishmen pushed on until Captain Wise actually reached the loopholed house and, taking a rifle from one of the dead, fired through the slits until he fell unconscious. C.S.M. McEvoy, a true son of Limerick, with all his company's officers killed or wounded led his men once more down the bullet-swept road shouting, 'Come on me boyos, the Irish never lost a Friday's battle yet.' 'D' Company under Captain Jervis attempted to break out over a railway cutting to the east of Etreux, but this too was lined with enemy infantry and the attack failed. Jervis was the last man to fall, seriously wounded,

Right: Major Paul Alfred Charrier.

firing his revolver at point blank range into von Barfeldt's massed infantry. Back on the road the artillerymen, including their troop commander Major Bayly, lay dead or injured around the last field gun. The machine-gun officer, Lieut. Chute, was killed at this point as he crossed the road with the intention of re-positioning the battalion's two guns.

'C' Company, the original rearguard, had at last been driven in by German infantry advancing from the north in overwhelming strength. The remainder of 'C' Company now joined survivors of the various attacks and fell back to an orchard on the west of the road. Major Charrier, 46 years of age, the oldest man present and a veteran of campaigns in East, West and

South Africa, had fought his last fight and Captain Hall of 'A' Company took command. Despite a further bayonet charge, at odds of one to fifty which had temporarily held the enemy, the orchard was now ringed by Germans against whom the surviving Munsters, lining the four sides of the orchard, made every shot count. About this time Captain Hall was severely wounded and command of the battalion passed to the senior subaltern, Lieut. Gower.

By this time it was growing dark and for the first time since early morning the machine-guns fell silent. The last cartridge had been fired and Sergeant Johnson, the machine-gun N.C.O., took his cherished guns in turn and smashed them in the light of flames from burning houses. Gradually the Germans edged forward, bringing more machine-guns into action, and at 9.15 p.m. four officers and 256 men of the Munsters, nearly out of ammunition and with many of them wounded, were overpowered. By now Lomax's Division was safely twelve miles away to the south and in the words of the Official History (referring to the 2nd Munsters) '...their heroic sacrifice had not been in vain.' Eight officers and 110 other ranks of the Munsters were buried in the orchard where they fell. German casualties, especially

Below: The action at Etreux, August 27th 1914.

earlier in the day, are not known but certainly 1,500 wounded were assembled in Etreux the next day, and this number without counting the dead.

Not all the Munsters at Etreux remained in German hands. A complete platoon, aided by the troop of 15th Hussars, slipped through the net before the final phase. Six more men, who apparently feigned death in the orchard, eventually made their way through Belgium into Holland and thence by ship to England. One of them, 9931 Private Donovan, finally returned to his reconstituted battalion on the Western Front exactly a year after Etreux. None of these men received any reward for their efforts, although Donovan won a Military Medal later on in the war.

In 1919, following a proposal to erect a Regimental Memorial at Etreux, the Battle Exploits Memorial Committee wrote as follows: 'The action is likely to become the classical example of the performance of its functions by a rearguard. The Battalion not only held up the attack of a strong hostile force in its original position, thereby securing the unmolested withdrawal of its Division, but in retiring drew on to itself the attacks of very superior numbers of the enemy. It was finally cut off at Etreux... but held out for several hours, the remnant only surrendering when their ammunition was practically exhausted and only a small number of men remained unhurt... No other claim to a memorial near Etreux is likely to be advanced - certainly nothing which would not take second place to the Munsters.'

Under Army Order 193 the following awards for gallantry in the field were granted to officers and men of the 2nd Munsters who were taken at Etreux. The ranks shown are those held in 1919 and not 1914.

M.C.
Lieut. Colonel H. S. Jervis
Major D. Wise

D.C.M.
4366 R.S.M. P. Cullinan (a)
5736 C.S.M. J. Browne
5911 Sergeant T. Foley (b)

M.M.
5829 C.S.M. P. McEvoy
6570 Sergeant W. Foley
9118 Sergeant G. Johnson
9264 Corporal R. Padfield

M.I.D.
Captain C. V. Deane-Drake
9059 L/Corporal E. J. Forward
9651 Sergeant D. Fountaine
7734 Sergt. (T/CQMS) C. Lister
Major C. R. Rawlinson

Above: Two views of the Etreux War memorial to the Munsters.

(a) The *London Gazette* of 12th December 1919, in an entry not connected with Army Order 193, carries a column of names of soldiers awarded the Meritorious Service Medal 'For Services in the War.' Among the recipients is R.S.M. Cullinan who spent 4½ years in captivity after being wounded and taken prisoner at Etreux. In the circumstances it is difficult to visualise what services he could have given, other than those in a prisoner of war camp.

(b) A large number of D.C.M. citations appear in the *London Gazette* of 14th April 1920 to recipients whose names have been listed in previous *Gazettes*. Three of these citations refer to acts of gallantry performed in 1914 by men of different regiments, all of whom were taken prisoner in the first year of the war. The three names first appeared in the L.G. of 12th December 1919 under a heading, 'For distinguished service in connection with Military Operations in France and Flanders.' One of the three men is 5911 Sergt. T Foley whose ninety-five word citation (in the 1920 *Gazette*) begins, 'For conspicuous gallantry on the 27th August 1914 during the rearguard action from Fesmy to

Etreux.' In common with Cullinan's M.S.M. there is nothing to indicate, in either *Gazette*, that the awards were made under the provisions of Army Order 193.

Decorations for escaping were gazetted as follows:

Captain Charles Hall recovered from his wounds and after two unsuccessful attempts to escape, which earned him a mention in despatches, made his third and successful attempt in 1917 and managed to cross the frontier into Switzerland. His D.S.O. for this feat was gazetted on 30th January 1920 also under A.O.193.

Privates 7761 Metcalfe and 7971 Young also escaped, apparently together, from their prisoner of war camp, and each was awarded a Military Medal.

For 'valuable services whilst a prisoner of war ' 9990 Pte. Jordan was mentioned in despatches. Under this heading, 5736 C.S.M. Browne who received a D.C.M. for his bravery at Etreux also received a M.I.D. for valuable services.

The 2nd Munsters was reconstituted on 9th November 1914 from substantial drafts and recovered sick and wounded. The battalion kept its identity until 19th April 1918 when, as the result of heavy losses sustained during the German spring offensive, it was amalgamated with the 1st battalion (of Gallipoli fame).

Alas the Royal Munster Fusiliers, in common with the other southern Irish regiments, was disbanded in 1922.

6
Last Stand at Reutel
2nd Wiltshires, First Ypres, October 1914

The Wiltshire Regiment's 2nd Battalion sailed from Gibraltar, its peacetime station, at the end of August 1914 and landed in England where it became part of the 7th Division which was still being formed. On 7th October 1914 the Division landed in Belgium at Zeebrugge to assist in the defence of Antwerp but the town fell to the Germans two days later whilst the Wiltshires, part of the 21st Infantry Brigade, were still moving up through Bruges. The brigade fell back to Ostend but four days later that town was also captured and the Wiltshires were the last British troops to leave the resort as the Germans entered close on their heels. Enemy forces were now advancing in great strength towards the remaining Channel ports and the 7th Division was sent to hold a line east of Ypres, pending the arrival of the main British Army from France.

On 14th October, after marching all night, the Wiltshires reached Ypres from where they moved forward through Hooge and halted; three days later they were astride the road in the Reutel/Becelaere sector some six miles east of Ypres. Here, in the afternoon, the battalion lost its first officer to enemy action when Captain Magor was killed in a clash with German cavalry. A patrol under Lieut. Ansted established that Germans were in Terhand, a village two miles southeast of Becelaere, but the enemy withdrew and the place was occupied by the Wiltshires when the 7th Division advanced on the 18th. While digging-in beyond the village the battalion was shelled from the south and suffered its first casualties from German artillery. Next day it was learned that the British position was threatened by an

Below: Captain Arthur Curgenven Magor.

50

entire enemy army corps and the Division fell back to its original line, covered by the Wiltshires, who did not get back to Reutel until after dark.

At this stage the precise whereabouts and movement of German forces was unknown (not unusual in 1914) and on 20th October the battalion once more set out for Terhand to cover the left flank of the 22nd Infantry Brigade which was to make a reconnaissance in force. As the Wiltshires' leading platoon topped a rise near the village they came under rifle fire and the platoon commander, Lieut. Spencer, was killed. Then came an urgent order from Divisional H.Q. that the forward troops were to withdraw at once and by nightfall the battalion was back in Reutel.

Twice during the night the Germans attacked in force but the Wiltshire's fifteen rounds a minute drove them off. All next day the battalion was heavily shelled; Lieut. Grimston was killed and casualties began to mount. Unfortunately, British artillery was scarce on the ground, and short of ammunition, and their counter-battery fire gradually weakened as the day wore on.

Below: Captain Horace Sylvester Grimston.

That afternoon an order was received from Brigade that the Wiltshires were to hold their position, including the hamlet of Reutel and a plateau to the south of it, 'at all costs.'

Towards dusk enemy infantry attacked in successive waves only to be mown down by concentrated rifle and machine-gun fire, but after dark the German guns registered on the battalion's rear positions. As a result, Capt. Henslow, in reserve with his company, and ably assisted by one of his sergeants with the unusual surname of Looney, experienced great difficulty and lost men from shell fire in getting food and ammunition to the men exposed on the plateau. During the night the brigade on the left, weakened by numerous casualties, was forced to fall back and Captain le Huquet and the Wiltshires' last reserves were forced to dig-in amid bursting shells in order to protect the exposed flank. Dawn on the 22nd October found the men spread out in one thin line with many of their rifles damaged by days of near

51

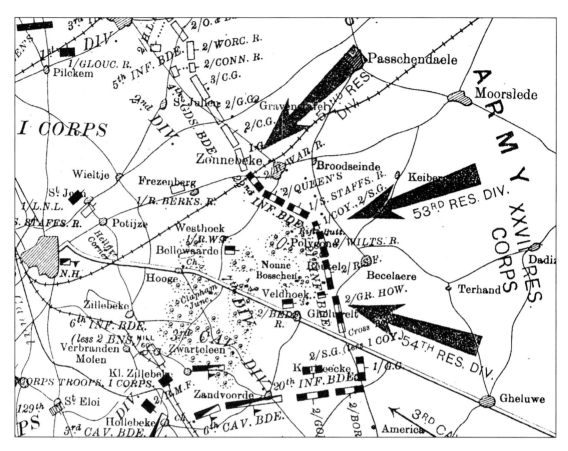

Above: The line at Reutel and environs, 22nd October 1914.

continuous rapid fire and by dirt and sand from bursting explosives. This day was to be a repetition of the previous one, with repeated attacks by enemy infantry, and their field artillery being moved even closer to Reutel.

By the morning of the 23rd many of the trenches, which were only shallow to start with, had been destroyed by shell-fire and the two machine-gun positions had been hit wrecking one gun and damaging the other, which reduced its rate of fire. In addition the water cart had been destroyed and the men's water bottles had been empty for over a day and there was no water even for the wounded, of whom there were many. The situation was especially vulnerable on the left flank and Captain Henslow was sent to Brigade to explain the circumstances and also to ask for 100 rifles. Meanwhile rumours passed from trench to trench that a retirement was imminent but a lull in the fighting enabled the C.O., Lieut. Colonel Forbes, to inform each company that no retirement would take place without a written order from him. The source of this misleading information appears to have originated with some stragglers in British uniforms who may have been German agents. As the result of Henslow's visit to Brigade H.Q. reinforcements arrived in the shape of a small party of South Staffords, who lost heavily while making their way into Reutel, and three under-strength platoons of Scots Guards.

On the 24th, while it was still dark, German artillery opened up with a devastating bombardment which pulverised what was left of the Wiltshire trenches. At 5 a.m. three battalions of the 244th German Reserve Infantry Regiment formed up ready to advance from the direction of Becelaere. The attackers would be guided onto their objective, Reutel, by the trees of Polygon Wood which stood directly behind the hamlet. Only the shells of cottages, one of which was on fire, marked the position of Reutel itself. In the half light enemy columns rolled forward still covered by a barrage from their artillery. However, either one formation was too early onto its target, or the German gunners were late in ceasing fire, for the men of the left-hand assaulting battalion reached the outskirts of Reutel in the midst of their own shelling and began a frontal attack on the 2nd Wiltshires.

The right-hand battalion advanced unopposed until it reached the trenches manned by the survivors of the Scots Guards who were crouched dazed among their dead, having received a number of direct hits from heavy howitzer shells. Overrunning this position allowed the attackers to start working down behind the Wiltshire along the edge of Polygon Wood. An isolated company of the Royal Scots Fusiliers, which was on the Wiltshires' right, was wiped out by 6 a.m. and the Germans took Reutel and swarmed in large numbers on the Wiltshire front, right flank and rear. Shortly afterwards another enemy column supported by machine-guns and artillery debouched from the ruins of Reutel and mopped-up the remaining defenders, working their way from right to left. Men were shot down from three sides and resistance collapsed. The C.O. and the adjutant, Captain Carver, had already been captured as they tried to find out what was happening on their right flank.

The 2nd Wiltshires had landed in Belgium on 7th October fielding a strength of 1,100 all ranks and now, just 19 days later, some 28 officers and 850 other ranks had been killed, wounded or captured. In fact the only two officers left were 2/Lieut. Waylen who had actually been promoted on the field from sergeant major while the battle was in progress, and the quartermaster, Lieut. Hewitt.

Meanwhile the commander of the bloodied but triumphant German 244th placed one battalion in Reutel and waited while the rest of his units reformed, buried the dead, and sent the wounded and prisoners to the rear. He was not aware that his regiment had torn a gap in the British defence line which would remain open for over two hours. Such an opportunity was never to be repeated.

Post-war awards under Army Order 193 to officers and men of the battalion for the action at Reutel were as follows:

Gallantry in the field:
M.C.
Captain Henslow.
D.C.M.
5342 Sgt. Looney.
M.I.D.
Captains Macnamara and R. Smith. 5125 L/Cpl. Hunt (killed in action), Privates 6239 Mead (since killed), 5443 Nash and 5103 Perrett.

For escaping or attempting to escape from P.O.W. camp:
M.M.
Privates 7539 Coombs and 8143 Midwinter.
M.I.D.
7966 Cpl. Webb.

Valuable services whilst a P.O.W:
M.I.D.
Major Wyndham, 5639 C.S.M. Robbins, 9293 Pte. Wheeler.

7
The Key to Victory
2nd Lincolns at Neuve Chapelle, 10th March 1915, and Aubers Ridge, 9th May 1915

The 2nd Battalion, Lincolnshire Regiment, was stationed in Bermuda when war was declared and stayed on the island until the middle of September 1914 when it left for Halifax, Nova Scotia. From there it sailed in convoy to England where, in company with the 2nd Royal Berkshires, 1st Royal Irish Rifles and the 2nd Rifle Brigade, it formed the 25th Infantry Brigade in the newly assembled 8th Division. After three weeks spent training and re-equipping, the Lincolns landed at Le Havre on 6th November 1914 and moved into trenches near Laventie on the 14th. The weather was exceptionally severe and in addition to the usual hazards of trench warfare many of the men, fresh from West Indian sunshine, suffered frost bitten feet. On 1st March 1915 the battalion moved to Estaires for intensive training and supplying working parties each evening to the front line opposite Neuve Chapelle.

In October 1914 German forces in Artois had seized the Neuve Chapelle salient which then enabled them to fire on the British positions on both flanks. Now, in March 1915, the British proposed to recapture the village and press on to take Aubers Ridge some 1½ miles north-east of Neuve Chapelle. Although the ridge only rose to the height of some 70 feet it was sufficient to dominate the flatlands of the Lys valley. In addition, if the town of Aubers itself could be taken it would threaten vital German road and rail communications between La Bassée and Lille. This was to be the first major offensive of the war launched from a trench system and it would be backed by some 340 guns, an unprecedented number at that stage of the war. As another first, the enemy's barbed wire was to be cut by artillery fire.

A fairly elaborate artillery fire plan was prepared and at 7.30 a.m. there would be a single round fired from 'Grannie,' a huge 15-inch howitzer bedded down at Sailly-Labourse. This would signal the first phase of the bombardment which was to last 35 minutes during which time the 18-pdrs., firing shrapnel, were

to cut passages through the enemy's wire, while other guns shelled the opposing trenches. At 8.05 a.m. 'Grannie' would signal the start of the second stage which included the assaulting infantry going over the top. At the same time selected batteries would shift their fire from the German forward trenches onto the village, and strong points to the north and south, while 9.2-inch and 6-inch howitzers would concentrate on Neuve Chapelle. During the same period 13- and 18-pdrs. would lay a screen of fire east of the village to make life difficult for any enemy reinforcements.

At 8 p.m. on 9th March the Lincolns moved to their battle stations with 'C' Company (Capt. Eagar) in the firing trench and breastworks on the right, and 'D' led by Capt. Bastard on the left. 'A' and 'B' Companies, supporting respectively 'C' and 'D' were about 150 yards to the rear in the assembly trenches. The attacking force consisted of four brigades and the 25th Brigade's frontage was some 400 yards in length and extended from the Rue Tilleloy-Neuve Chapelle road to the north of Sign

Above: 'Grannie' - a 15-inch breech loading howitzer shown siege mounted on a ground platform. Fired a 1400 lb high explosive projectile with a maximum range of 10,795 yards. Manned by detachments of Royal Marine Artillery until 1916 when these weapons were handed over to the Army. Required a crew of twelve.

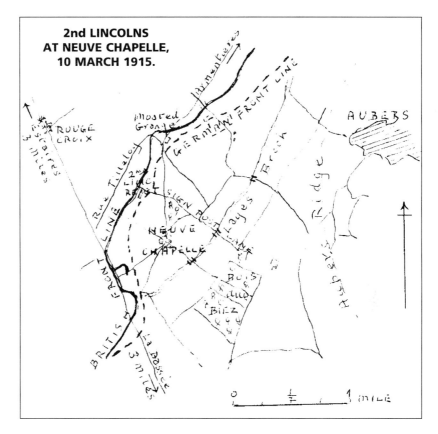

Post Lane. An Indian formation, the Dehra Dun Brigade, was on the right of the 25th with the 23rd Infantry Brigade on the left. During the evening the Corps Commander issued a Special Order to the troops which read: 'The attack which we are about to undertake is of the first importance to the Allied cause. The Army and the Nation are watching the result and Sir John French (the C-in-C) is confident that every individual in the IV Corps will do his duty and inflict a crushing defeat on the German VII Corps which is opposed to us.' Not surprisingly this stimulating message did not mention that two of the 6-inch howitzer batteries had only moved into position the previous day and the crews had not bedded down the guns or had time to register their target, which was the enemy wire in front of the 23rd Brigade - the 25th's left-hand neighbours.

Punctually at 7.30 a.m. the barrage crashed down on the German lines. The wire entanglements, which varied in depth from six to 15 yards were being blown to bits along the whole front, with the exception of about 400 yards in front of the 23rd

Brigade. At the same time the enemy trenches and their occupants were practically obliterated. While the Lincolns watched the wholesale destruction of the enemy opposite they also suffered a considerable number of casualties from our own guns dropping 'shorts.' The P.B.I. were convinced that Sod's Law dictated that most of the duds always fell on the enemy but the 'shorts' falling on our own men usually exploded.

It was almost a relief when 'Grannie' signalled the second phase and 'C' and 'D' Companies went over the breastworks and across No-Man's-Land. One enemy machine-gun, manned by two wounded German officers, and a number of riflemen had survived the carnage, but these were quickly overcome for the loss of about 20 men. Capt. Bastard was the first man into the enemy firing trench, closely followed by Capt. Peake and his bombing party whose instructions were to block the enemy trench at Sign Post Lane until the 23rd Brigade was in touch. Holding aloft a blue flag (indicating a blocking party) Capt. Peake and his men rushed along the trench to the left driving about 30 Germans before them in a running fight. Their retreat was cut off when men of the 23rd came up and the fleeing troops were made captive. It was at this point that Capt. Peake,

Left: Neuve Chapelle. Waiting for the attack

having ordered a German officer who had surrendered to remove his equipment and lay down his arms, turned his head for a moment to speak to one of his N.C.O.s. The German thereupon twice fired his revolver at his captor at point blank range. As Peake fell dead the German was bayoneted by every Lincoln man who could reach him.

Meanwhile the support companies had followed hard on the heels of 'C' and 'D' and entered the German lines from which the enemy now appeared to be in full retreat. Greatly elated the Lincolns pushed on over the communications trenches and even the injured tried to follow their comrades. L/Cpl. Perry, badly wounded in the foot, was ordered three times to take cover but, although hampered by a Barr and Stroud rangefinder, he insisted on rallying his men. (He was later mentioned in despatches). Sadly, between the first and second enemy lines, the C.O., Lt. Col. McAndrew, fell and shortly died, with his right leg practically blown off by a shell.

The two forward companies, joined by some of 'A' Company, continued to advance until they reached a wide and deep watercourse, probably a dyke, which was not shown on any of their maps. The obstacle was temporarily bridged and the onward momentum continued until they ran into a curtain of fire from their own guns and the officers decided to fall back and entrench on the other side of the water. As they began to re-cross the dyke one of the subalterns, Lieut. Wylie, was shot and mortally wounded by a German sniper wearing a British uniform and firing from the left rear.

Elsewhere the attacking troops had met with mixed fortunes. On the left, the two leading battalions of the 23rd Brigade (2nd Scottish Rifles and the 2nd Middlesex) found that the enemy wire and trenches in front of them had not been seriously damaged and the men had to tear their way through the barbed wire with their bare hands. Both battalions suffered hideous casualties ('A', 'B' and 'C' Companies of the Middlesex were practically wiped out) but managed to take their objectives. On the other end of the line the two leading companies of the 1/39th Garhwalis lost direction and veered onto untouched German defences. They also tackled the wire with bare hands and eventually gained the enemy trench at the expense of many killed, including all their British officers.

Nevertheless, Neuve Chapelle with its fortified houses and numerous machine-guns had been captured, British and Indian infantry had advanced some 1,200 yards on a front of 4,000 yards, and the way to Aubers Ridge lay open. However, German positions north and south the captured ground were still intact and the Corps Commander elected to hold back the untouched 7th Division in case of a counter-attack. Furthermore, communications had broken down at every level between front line units and Corps H.Q. and there was a delay of five hours before the reserve brigades of 8th Division were in a position to resume the offensive. By that time it was too late. Under cover of dusk German reinforcements prepared a second line defence and leading enemy troops had already infiltrated the Bois du Biez from the east.

Renewed efforts by the British on thc 10th and 11th failed to make material progress and neither did a full scale British assault on the 12th nor the German counter-attack later the same day. This was the last day of the battle and that evening the troops were ordered to consolidate the ground already taken. The 2nd Lincolns first big action had cost the battalion 15 officers and 298 other ranks killed and wounded, but the survivors had not heard the last of Aubers Ridge.

Confident that the Battle of Neuve Chapelle had shown them the key to victory, (a savage artillery bombardment which destroyed enemy defences and demoralised the defenders) the British High Command now proposed to take Aubers Ridge. The Indian and I Corps would attack south of Neuve Chapelle and the 7th and 8th Divisions of IV Corps to the north of the village. Having breached the German line at two points some 6,000 yards apart, the two attacking formations would bend in and isolate the enemy on the Ridge. The 25th Infantry Brigade, to which had been added the 13th (County of London) Bn. were on the extreme left of the British onslaught. Brigade frontage was about 700 yards and ran from the Sailly-Fromelles road on the right, which divided it from 24th Brigade, to a road on the left which ran from La Cordonnerie Farm and past Delangre Farm.

On 9th May 1915 at 5.40 a.m. after a bombardment limited to 40 minutes because of a severe shortage of shells, the assaulting infantry went over the top. In the 25th Brigade sector the Rifle Brigade led on the right, supported by the Berkshires, and the Lincolns followed the Royal Irish Rifles on the left. The 13th Londoners were 400 yards further to the left where two mines were to be detonated under the German trenches. As the leading waves moved into No-Man's-Land they were subjected to fierce artillery and machine-gun fire and it became obvious that the 40 minute barrage had neither neutralised the defence nor adequately cut the enemy wire. Despite heavy casualties the survivors of the foremost battalions stormed the first line of German breastworks and pressed on to their final objective 200 yards away, the Fromelles road.

'A' and 'B,' the two leading Lincoln companies, reached the enemy firing trench as the volume of German fire rose to a crescendo and the advancing troops were pinned down and unable to move. By this time the Lincoln support companies, 'C' and 'D,' had reached the British parapet and were ordered by Brigadier General Lowry Cole to work their way across No-Man's-Land and take the German trench to the west of the 13th Londoners. The latter were occupying the craters formed by the explosion of the two mines. At that point, according to the *Official History*, (Vol.IV. p.36) 'a number of men of the Rifle Brigade and Irish Rifles were seen streaming back over the German breastworks bringing with them the other two companies ('A' and 'B') of the 2nd Lincolnshires.' Some unauthorised person had given the order to retire. The Brigadier jumped up onto the parapet and by voice and gesture succeeded in stopping the

Right: 2nd Lincolns at Aubers Ridge, 9th May 1915.

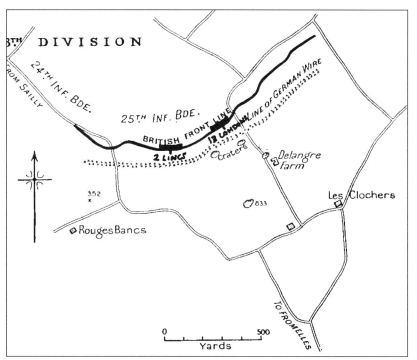

withdrawal, but attempts to resume the advance foundered in the face of the murderous fire sweeping No-Man's-Land. The Brigadier was still standing up in the open encouraging his men when he was shot dead.

The action now became a soldiers' battle with the attackers split into separate groups. Capt. Thruston and 'C' Company gained the objective and were preceded by a blocking and bombing party in which Corporal Sharpe won the Victoria Cross. In the words of the *London Gazette* dated 29th June 1915, 'He was the first to reach the enemy's position and using bombs with great determination and effect, he himself cleared them out of a trench fifty yards long. By this time all his party had fallen and he was then joined by four other men, with whom he attacked the enemy again with bombs, and captured a further trench two hundred and fifty yards long.' Privates Bills, Donderdale and Leeman, the men who backed Sharpe (the fourth man was killed) were each awarded the D.C.M.

Elsewhere on the field, Sergeant Brocklesby took command of a party of men lying in the open, leaderless, and exposed to very heavy machine-gun and rifle fire, and succeeded in leading them forward to reinforce a group already holding a German trench. He was severely wounded and he also was given a well earned D.C.M. Another sergeant, Clarke, gained the D.C.M. for leading his platoon losing many men in so doing, to the assistance of some Royal Irish in another part of an enemy trench. Later he went out under heavy fire and cut the German barbed wire, enabling his men to retire. Another D.C.M. went to Pte. Cowling who covered the withdrawal of his section by holding up the enemy in hand to hand fighting. He killed several until his rifle was torn out of his hands by his infuriated opponents struggling to get at him. Then, against all the odds, he made good his escape amid a positive hail of bullets. The action for which Pte. Kirby earned the D.C.M. was in one of the mine craters in which 15 wounded Lincolns and about 100 13th Londoners were taking cover. A German threw a lighted bomb into the middle of them, but before it could burst Kirby picked it up and threw it back.

By 9 a.m. men were being dribbled across No-Man's-Land to reinforce defenders in various parts of the German trench system but few of them ever reached their objective, the majority were shot down. Capt. Thruston was still holding on and at one point located two enemy machine-guns firing from beyond the craters and organised a bombing party to silence them. At 10.30 a.m. he reported that he was in possession of the enemy trench to the west of the mine craters and was awaiting further orders. However, communications had broken down, as usual, and runners were unable to reach him as the ground was being smothered by enfilade machine-gun fire from hostile trenches to the north east (untouched by the barrage). It was 4 p.m. before a written order reached him to withdraw his men and even then it was impossible to move during daylight and it was not until four hours later that he began to retire. As his party began to move they were attacked from both flanks, the rear, and from the crater on his left front. All the bombs had been expended, the machine-guns damaged or destroyed, and Thruston ordered 'every man for himself' to break out towards their own parapet. Thruston was awarded the D.S.O. and survived the war, but not the influenza epidemic in November 1918. A party of 'A' Company which had apparently been lying in front of the German wire all day also withdrew to their own trenches under cover of darkness. Most of 'D' Company appear to have perished in No-Man's-Land.

That night the 25th Brigade was relieved by the 23rd and moved back to the rear. The Battle of Aubers Ridge had cost the British Army 458 officers and 11,161 men killed, wounded and missing and had cost the 2nd Lincolns nine officers and 200 other ranks killed and wounded and 77 rank and file missing. One of the missing, C.Q.M.S. Smith, wounded and taken prisoner, was later awarded the M.M. under the terms of Army Order 193 for escaping from his prisoner of war camp.

Aubers Ridge was eventually taken - in September 1918.

8
The Invincible Eight
2nd East Surreys at Neuve Chapelle, 12th March 1915

The 12th March 1915 was an unfortunate day for the 2nd Battalion East Surrey Regiment, which suffered nearly a 100 casualties in a side-show of the Battle of Neuve Chapelle in which it had only a supporting role. Men of the 7th Infantry Brigade were to pass through the three trenches held by the battalion in order to attack and capture Spanbroek Molen. The assaulting infantry would only be briefly exposed in No-Man's-Land as the German trenches at this point were less than thirty yards away from the East Surreys; who would cover the advance with rapid fire and rifle grenades.

Unfortunately the day dawned with thick mist and the one hour and forty minutes bombardment of the enemy positions, originally timed to start at 7 a.m. did not begin until 2.30 p.m. Thus the attack was postponed from 8.40 a.m. until 4.10 p.m. Owing to the close proximity of the enemy front line to British positions the Surrey's left hand trench was evacuated at dawn, as ordered, in case of 'shorts' (known these days as 'friendly fire') from our own guns. The right-hand trench was still manned and became very crowded owing to some of the attacking force having worked their way into it ready to go over the top.

This right-hand section was heavily shelled by the enemy and also swept by the fire of two German machine-guns sited on its right front. As a result the trench became choked with dead and wounded of the East Surrey garrison together with troops of the assault brigade. Two Surrey 2/Lieutenants, Becker and de Buriatte, were among the slain. The trench also came under fire from British artillery and the remaining officer, 2/Lieut. Kirkland, ordered

Below: Captain John Philip De Buriatte.

the unwounded survivors to retire. As the party disengaged Kirkland was killed by a rifle bullet and there were serious losses among the men.

Sgt. Alfred Bull and four men, all of them wounded, were all that remained of the four officers and 85 rank and file who had originally manned the position. The sergeant and his men were on the extreme right of the trench and busy engaging the two German machine-gun crews. Hence they did not hear, or ignored, the order to withdraw. Brigade H.Q. was informed that the battalion was being heavily shelled by our own guns, but as the message was being passed the telephone line was cut by a shell. The officer commanding battalion supports, fearing that the trench might be rushed by the enemy, ordered 2/Lieut. Crabb with 25 men to reoccupy it. This group had nearly reached its objective when another machine-gun opened up on them killing or wounding all but three. Crabb was among the dead, shot through the head.

Below: 'The Invincible Eight' 2nd East Surreys at Neuve Chapelle (*Deeds that Thrill the Empire*).

It was obviously impossible to reinforce the trench during the hours of daylight and thus for several hours Sgt. Bull and his seven men held the position under a hail of high explosives as well as machine-gun and rifle fire. Many parts of the trench and parapet had been demolished by shell fire and what was left of the trench was encumbered with the dead and dying. At any minute the small party expected the Germans to rush them in overwhelming numbers, but the volume of fire from the Surrey stalwarts presumably convinced their opponents that the trench was still held by a powerful body of troops. When darkness fell the invincible eight were relieved by a platoon from their battalion.

Later that month, Sgt. Bull and two of the original surviving defenders of the trench, Privates A. J. Doyle and F. Ruffell, were each decorated with the D.C.M. by the Major General commanding 3rd Division, for their gallantry on the 12th.

9
The Mound of Death
4th Rifle Brigade, St. Eloi,
15th March 1915

The 4th Battalion, Rifle Brigade, was stationed in India when Britain declared war and the unit did not land in France until 21st December 1914. Thus the riflemen were fortunate to miss the early battles on the Western Front in which so many of the regular infantry regiments of the B.E.F. were nearly destroyed. However, during the early months of 1915 the battalion saw its fair share of trench warfare (and attendant casualties) but on 14th March 1915 the officers and men were resting behind the lines in billets about three miles from Poperinghe. That evening the Rifles together with the rest of the 80th Infantry Brigade, comprising the 3rd Battalion, King's Royal Rifle Corps, 2nd Bn. King's Shropshire Light Infantry and Princess Patricia's Canadian Light Infantry, were suddenly stood to arms and hurried to Dickebusch, about three miles west of St. Eloi.

St. Eloi was a village standing on rising ground and situated at an important X shaped junction of the main roads to Ypres and Voormezeele. The enemy held the high ground behind St. Eloi, and his front line was about 400 yards southeast of the cross roads. Between this front line and the village, to the east of the Voormezeele road, stood a large artificial knoll known as the Mound which formed part of the defence structure. There were also ten forward posts numbered 13 to 22 and a number of supporting trenches sited on either side and in front of the village. There were also three barricades, one behind the other in St. Eloi itself and a redoubt and two strong points immediately behind the last buildings in the village.

At 5 p.m. on 14th March the Germans exploded a mine under the Mound and, supported by a violent artillery bombardment, rushed the posts and trenches, captured the Mound, and penetrated into the village. The 80th Infantry Brigade now moved up in support of the 82nd Infantry Brigade which was thrown into

ST ELOI. November 1915,

a hurried counter-attack, but by 3 a.m. on the 15th it became obvious that the cobbled attempt to recover the lost positions had failed. Now the 80th was given the task of restoring the situation and recapturing the Mound.

The Rifle Brigade was to mount the major attack by moving up from Voormezeele to St. Eloi along the main road as it was impossible to move across country owing to the waterlogged condition of the ground. The Princess Pats, backed by the K.R.R.C., were to co-operate by pushing along the other main road and attacking towards St. Eloi, clearing posts 19, 20 and 21 on the way - this would protect the riflemen's left flank - and the Shropshires (less one company) were sent in support of the Rifle Brigade.

In the event the P.P.C.L.I. was blocked on the road to Voormezeele and daylight was not far away. Therefore, at about 4.30 a.m., Colonel Thesiger, C.O. of the 4th, decided that his men would have to mount the attack without Canadian support. Leaving 'B' Company and the battalion 2nd i/c, Major A. M. King in reserve at Bus House the remainder of the 4th fixed swords (riflemen fix swords, infantrymen fix bayonets) and moved forward to the vicinity of S.9. 'D' Company under Capt. Mostyn Pryce set off to work round the south of the village and

Above: St Eloi, November 1915.

Top right: The action at St Eloi, 15th March 1915.

Right: Captain Hugh Beauclerk Mostyn Pryce.

68

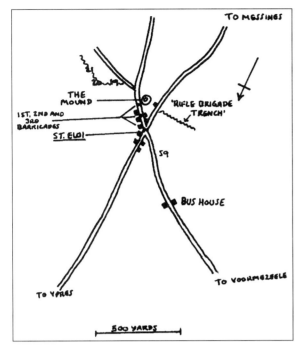

recapture Rifle Brigade Trench. Fifteen minutes later Capt. Selby-Smyth was to take 'C' Company and leap frog by platoons to clear the barricades and their defenders, push on through St. Eloi, and take the Mound and the old front line. 'A' Company would follow 'C' into the village and clear any pockets of resistance left in the houses.

This plan was a tall order by any standard and only an element of surprise plus the fact that the men were well-trained regular troops enabled them to come within a whisker of success. According to the transport officer writing in the *Rifle Brigade Chronicle* for 1926, there was 'no information, no artillery support, no facility for covering fire, confusion and obstruction by other units and a night attack up a street swept by machine-gun fire.'

Swooping out of the darkness onto Rifle Brigade trench, 'D' Company scattered the startled garrison who fled, leaving behind them their kit, rations and half-cooked breakfasts. Casualties were light except among the officers. Captain Pryce was shot in the head by a German sniper firing from the Mound and 2/Lieut. John Stobart was killed as he led his platoon into action. Pryce was the last direct representative of one of the oldest county families in Wales and had only recently refused a commission as a major in the newly formed Welsh Guards. A regular soldier, he had served with the battalion in the South African War 1899-1902, unlike young Stobart who had only joined the regiment six weeks previously.

'C' Company raced into the village but the leading platoon came under heavy fire from the first barricade, situated at the cross roads near the centre of St. Eloi, and the company commander Captain Selby-Smyth, was killed leading his men against the obstacle and its defenders. Another regular soldier, he had served with the Rifle Brigade in Egypt and India apart from a two-year stint as A.D.C. to the Governor of Western Australia. At this point Colonel Thesiger sent in the reserve of 'C' Company who rushed the barricade and pushed forward until they were pinned down by accurate fire from the second barricade which had been built some 50 yards down the Warncton road in the direction of the Mound. This second obstacle was stormed by 'A' Company which pressed forward until it came under still heavier fire from the third barricade across the road beside the Mound, and from the Mound itself which by now had been converted into a nest of machine-guns.

'Repeated efforts were made by individual officers and men to rush forward, but the sting had gone out of the attack,' wrote Col. Thesiger in his report. By this time the attackers position was being swept by the guns on the Mound and faint daylight was helping the German machine-gunners. The C.O., who had established his advanced headquarters at the second barricade, now sent the adjutant to bring up the reserve company.

The adjutant reached Bus House at 5.15 a.m. and 'B' Company set off at the double for St. Eloi. Meanwhile the confusion in the outskirts of the village was indescribable. Remnants of the 82nd Brigade, which had been repulsed earlier that morning, were trying to make their way back and were mixed up with the Shropshires who were moving up to support the Rifle Brigade. Meanwhile, most of two companies of the Shropshires managed to struggle through the press of troops on the only usable road and reported themselves to Colonel Thesiger. He in turn, with the arrival of 'B' Company, hoping to take the last objective before it was fully daylight, hurriedly organised a general advance against the Mound, but it was too late. Major King, who led the assault, was immediately killed although 2/Lieut. Ritchie succeeded in reaching the Mound, followed by an unknown sergeant and rifleman plus Captain Vassar-Smith of the Shropshires. Both officers were shot dead. Ritchie, still four months short of his 21st birthday, was seen to fall into a trench at the foot of the Mound, and Vassar-Smith lay in the roadway. Lieut. Stopford-Sackville and a rifleman worked their

Right: Temp. Major-General George Handcock Thesiger C.B., C.M.G. (as a captain, c.1902). Killed in command of the 9th (Scottish) Division at Loos, 26th September 1915

way along the buildings on the left of the road until they reached the last house and from there, the officer using his revolver, started shooting at the enemy machine-gunners firing from the Mound. Stopford-Sackville, known to his intimates as 'Tiger' was the son of a former C.O. of the 4th Battalion.

Awarded the D.S.O. for his bravery at St. Eloi he was invalided as a major in 1919. Sadly he died in 1920 of slow paralysis at the young age of 26.

By now it was 6 a.m. and almost broad daylight, and casualties were mounting among the congested mass of troops by the St. Eloi cross roads. It was obvious that the Mound would never be taken without heavy artillery preparation and the attacking troops were withdrawn. The battalion had suffered six officers and 28 other ranks killed and died of wounds, four officers and 59 rank and file wounded, and six missing; a modest casualty list considering the task they had been given and in which they had so nearly succeeded. Lieut. Hargreaves, the battalion bombing and sniping officer, was among the wounded and left lying out in the road below the Mound when the brigade withdrew. An order was issued that no-one was to search for the wounded as too many men had been lost when looking for fallen comrades. Ignoring this prohibition four of Hargreaves' snipers went to St. Eloi on the following night and managed to bring him in on a makeshift stretcher. He was incapable of moving by himself as he had been shot through the lungs and right leg; his left arm was broken and his left foot and right hand had been shattered by shrapnel. He was awarded an immediate Military Cross for his part in the action and recovered from his multiple wounds to return to the active list. Promoted to captain in 1915 he spent the last two years of the war as adjutant to the 11th Royal Tank Corps in France. Invalided out of the service in 1922 he still contrived to serve as a wing commander in the R.A.F. Volunteer Reserve during the whole of World War II.

In addition to awards to officers and mentions in despatches, C.S.M. Saunders (wounded three times but still encouraging his men) and C.S.M. Tait received the D.C.M., as did Corporal Felgate who, although wounded, stayed all through the following day sniping from houses in the village at Germans on the Mound.

None of the Rifle Brigade officers of the 4th Battalion were ever taken as prisoners of war, whether wounded or not, either at St. Eloi or in any other engagement throughout the war.

10
Six V.C.s Before Breakfast
1st Lancashire Fusiliers, W Beach, Gallipoli, 25th April 1915

The Gallipoli campaign (Winston Churchill's brainchild) was mounted in order to force the Dardanelles and move into the Sea of Marmara to threaten, or take, Constantinople. Had this plan succeeded it would probably have knocked Turkey out of the war in one stroke. Unfortunately, a premature bombardment of the outer forts by a British naval force in November 1914 had alerted both the Turks and their German allies to the danger of an Allied landing on the peninsula.

In February 1915 an Anglo-French fleet, which included sixteen battleships, began the systematic reduction of the Turkish batteries and fortifications in an attempt to force the passage by the weight of naval power alone. But, on 18th March when the enemy was near the end of his resources, three Allied old battleships were sunk in an undetected minefield and three others disabled. The ten remaining capital ships were hastily withdrawn out of the Strait.

Meanwhile a British expeditionary force totalling 78,000 men, which included a French Division, was en route from England and Egypt. However, when the transports began to assemble at Mudros, the advance base, it was discovered that the vessels of the contingent from England had been haphazardly loaded. Thus on 25th March the ships had to sail back to Alexandria, in Egypt, where they were unloaded and then combat-stowed by unit, with the men, guns, ammunition and equipment all in the same ship. This delay gave the Turks five weeks grace which they used to improve the defences and, under the command of German General von Sanders, deploy some 60,000 troops on the peninsula. The enemy was now forewarned and forearmed.

The initial landings were made on 25th April 1915; by the Anzacs at Ari Burnu (Z Beach) north of Gaba Tepe on the western side of the peninsula, and the British 29th Division at five beaches designated S, V, W, X and Y. S Beach was on the

southern side, between Morto Bay and Eski Hissarlik Point, Y
was on the western side about 10 miles south of Z, and X, W and
V on Cape Helles proper. W Beach, a small sandy cove flanked

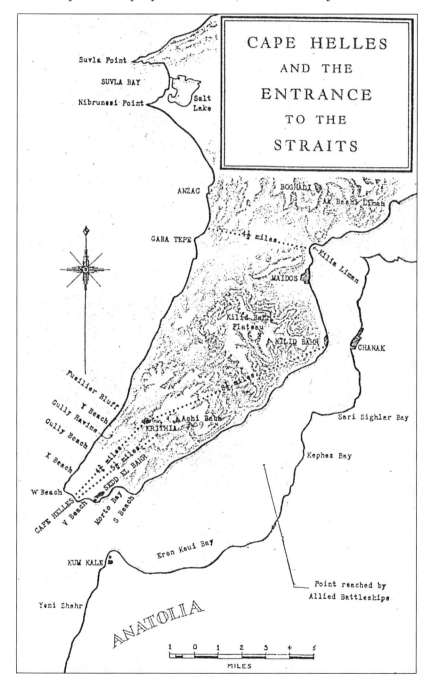

Left: Cape Helles and
the Entrance to the
Straits.

by steep cliffs, was allotted to the 1st Battalion, Lancashire Fusiliers, which was to spearhead the 86th Fusilier Brigade in seizing the landing place and then spreading out to link up with the other units landing at X and V on either side of it.

A belt of barbed wire, three rows deep and stretching the length of the 350 yards strip of beach, faced the Lancashires who were ordered to lie down once they hit the beach until the men with wire cutters had dealt with the obstruction. In addition, and unknown to the troops, there were submerged trip wires strung out beneath the water line and land mines sown on the shore. Three short trenches, one on each cliff and the other on a low ridge in the gully between them, covered the beach. More manned Turkish positions to the north and south commanded the ridge and machine-gun posts had been excavated into the cliff face. Two wired redoubts further inland were sited to contain any breakthrough towards Hill 138, an enemy position between W and V Beaches.

Most of the battalion was aboard HMS *Euryalus* an old armoured cruiser, which approached to within 200 yards of the shore, while 'D' Company with Battalion H.Q. and Brigade Headquarters were on HMS *Implacable*, a pre-Dreadnought battleship which anchored closer to the beach. At 6 a.m. after a 45 minute naval bombardment six picket boats, each towing four ship's cutters in line astern, left the shelter of HMS *Euryalus* and headed for the land. Once ashore, 'A' and 'B' Companies attacking

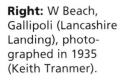

Right: W Beach, Gallipoli (Lancashire Landing), photographed in 1935 (Keith Tranmer).

on the right, commanded respectively by Captains Haworth and
Shaw, plus the battalion's machine-gun section, were to rush the
cliff top trenches and then push inland to capture Hill 138. 'C'
Company, led by Capt. Willis, on the left flank of the landing, was
to get through the wire and take the Turkish trenches on Hill 114
overlooking the centre and left-hand sectors of the beach. Having
disposed of those defenders the men would then incline half left
to join up with the units landed from X Beach. Two platoons from
'D' Company were to accompany 'C' as reserves, to be joined by
the remainder of the company plus Battalion H.Q. and Headquarters Company being ferried ashore from HMS *Implacable*.
Crammed in their boats, and laden down with full kit and equipment, including three days rations and 200 rounds of ammunition, the 1,002 Lancashire Fusiliers and their officers were about
to become part of military folklore.

The Peninsula was apparently deserted as the picket boat tows
were slipped and the five seamen in each cutter took to the oars.
Suddenly a single shot rang out from the cliffs - the starting gun
for a massacre. Exposed and helpless in their slow-moving boats
the attackers were literally sitting targets for the concealed
machine-guns and Turkish riflemen. About 100 yards from the
shore the troops went over the side into breast-high water and
began to struggle ashore through murderous fire being poured in
them from the front and either flank. The survivors were not
even able to retaliate as their rifles were clogged with a mixture
of sand and sea water. Still under close range fire those men who
had gained the beach huddled by the uncut wire and fumbled for
oil and pull through to clean their weapons. This could have
been avoided if the company commanders' request for breech
covers had been acted upon. The attack at this point had stalled
and over 350 casualties were strewn about on the beach or
floating in shallow water offshore.

Total disaster was only averted by the success of 'C' Company
on the left which had got ashore relatively unscathed. In addition some of the boats from the main party had been diverted
over towards the left where the beach was partly sheltered by a
cliff. Brigadier Hare personally led the attack which captured
Turkish trenches on Hill 114 but he was severely wounded an
hour later while making a reconnaissance towards X Beach. On
the right, 'A' Company's attempt to storm the right-hand cliff
was shattered by a heavy shell fired from one of the British
ships offshore, which fell short. Now the 50 remaining men of

Right: Captain Willis, with stick, rallies his men on W Beach.

the company were joined by 12 survivors from 'B' Company's first wave, plus Capt. Cunliffe who had been unable to land his machine-guns but had managed to swim ashore through the intense fire. Together with brigade major and staff captain this group moved off in an attempt to take Hill 138 from the south. The attack was baulked by a belt of unbroken wire and Capt. Frankland, the brigade major, was killed.

It was then that Pte. Bill Keneally took matters into his own hands and risked almost certain death in crawling forward through a hail of bullets and attempted to cut a path through the wire. The attempt was unsuccessful as the Government issue wirecutters broke and Keneally made his way back to the party, miraculously unscathed. The group remained in their precarious position until late afternoon when reinforcements arrived and the two redoubts were captured.

Elsewhere, all the Lancashires' objectives had been gained but at the cost of 178 rank and file killed and 520 wounded. Eleven officers, the R.S.M. and three C.S.M.s were among the fallen. Three pairs of brothers were also parted this day - but not for long. 2304 Pte. Sam Arney was among the dead and his brother, 2298 Pte. Bert Arney, died of his wounds five days later. 1307 Pte. William Brace was killed on the beach and his elder brother 777 L/Cpl. Alfred Brace was to be killed in action a month later. 1849 Pte. George Wickstead was among the slain and his brother, 1687 Pte. John Wickstead had only another six days to live. Captain Willis's men had borne some of the heaviest fighting of the day, both on the beach and during the taking of Hill 114, and his company was reduced to four officers and 83 men. The company signaller, L/Cpl. Grimshaw, had been a tower of strength and was unhurt although his pack and water bottle were riddled with bullets and another shot had smashed his cap badge and whipped the hat off his head. One of the survivors, Sgt. Alfred Richards, had just reached the beach when a burst of machine-gun fire almost severed his right leg. Despite the terrible pain he dragged his mangled limb through the barbed wire shouting encouragement to his men and trying to keep up with them as they attacked enemy positions. Another 'C' Company N.C.O., Sgt. Frank Stubbs, had led from the front urging his platoon through the wire and up the cliff. He was killed later that morning leading the troops to the crest of Hill 114.

Among the officers, Captains Willis, Haworth and the adjutant, Bromley, had all displayed outstanding bravery and leadership. Bromley, who had landed with H.Q. Company, had perhaps done more than anyone to get the men through the beach obstacles and up the cliffs. He was apparently admired by the whole battalion.

On 15th May Major General Sir Aylmer Hunter-Weston, commanding the 29th Division, wrote in a submission to G.H.Q., 'The landing is a deed of heroism that has seldom been equalled and I strongly recommend that the gallantry of the deed may be recognised by the bestowal of six V.C.s on the two most distinguished officers and the four most distinguished NCOs and men, namely Captains C. Bromley and R.R. Willis, Sergeants A. Richards and F.E. Stubbs, Cpl. J. Grimshaw and Pte. W. Keneally... Their deeds of heroism took place under my own eyes... Where all did so marvellously it is difficult to discriminate, but the opinion of the battalion is that Bromley and Willis are the officers, and Stubbs, Richards, Grimshaw and Keneally are the NCOs and men to whom perhaps the greatest credit is due. As the representatives, therefore of the battalion, as well as for the deeds of great gallantry performed by themselves ... I strongly recommend these officers, NCOs and men for the V.C.'

Sir Ian Hamilton, the G.O.C., endorsed the recommendation but it was scaled down by War Office red tape as the submission had not been made under Article 13 of the V.C. Warrant which allowed men of a unit or ship to ballot on behalf of their comrades. In the event three names were allowed and the

London Gazette of 23rd August 1915 announced the award of the Victoria Cross to Captain Richard Raymond Willis, No.1293 Sergeant Alfred Richards and No.1809 Private William Keneally, all of 1st Battalion Lancashire Fusiliers. Their joint citation read, 'On 25th April 1915, three Companies and the Headquarters of the 1st Battalion, Lancashire Fusiliers in effecting a landing on the Gallipoli Peninsula to the west of Cape Helles were met by a very deadly fire from hidden machine-guns, which caused a great number of casualties. The survivors, however, rushed up to and cut the wire entanglements, notwithstanding a terrific fire from the enemy, and, after overcoming supreme difficulties, the cliffs were gained and the position maintained. Amongst many very gallant officers and men engaged in this most hazardous enterprise, Captain Willis, Sergeant Richards and Private Keneally have been selected by their comrades as having performed most signal acts of bravery and devotion to duty.' Sadly, by the time this notice appeared, Keneally was already dead. Badly wounded in the Battle for Gully Ravine on 28th June he died the next day.

Captain Haworth received a D.S.O., L/Cpl. Grimshaw was awarded a D.C.M. and Bromley and Stubbs got nothing. However, Brigadier Owen Wolley-Dod, Hunter-Weston's general staff officer, was troubled by the apparent injustice to Bromley, Stubbs and Grimshaw and pressed for the case to be re-examined. The fact that he was an old Lancashire Fusilier may have sharpened the edge of his interest in the matter. His efforts were eventually successful but it was not until 15th March 1917 that the *London Gazette* announced the award of V.C.s to all three men. The citation was the same as that for the initial three Victoria Cross awards. By the time the notice appeared Bromley was dead and Grimshaw, now Sergeant Grimshaw, could not at first believe that the V.C. had been substituted for his D.C.M. At the time this was only the ninth occasion that a lesser award had been cancelled in favour of the V.C. Sgt. Stubbs of course had already been killed on the first day of the landings.

Sergeant Richards was a child of the regiment in which his father had served 21 years with the 2nd Battalion, rising to the rank of colour sergeant. After being wounded Richards was taken to Egypt where his mangled right leg was amputated above the knee. Evacuated to England he was discharged from the Army on 31st July 1915 as medically unfit; he had served 20 years with the regiment and held the long service and good conduct medal. Despite his artificial leg he served with the Home Guard throughout W.W.II. He died in 1953 after a short illness.

Grimshaw was 22 years of age when he landed on W Beach and died in 1980 at the ripe old age of 87. He escaped being wounded on the peninsula but fell victim to frostbite and spent five weeks in hospital in Egypt before convalescence in England. Sent to France in 1916 he was commissioned in the field and in 1918 posted to India where he served with the 1/75th Carnatic Infantry in the sub-continent and Arabia. He rejoined his regiment in Ireland in 1921 just in time for the troubles. After retiring from the Army he served as a recruiting officer in Cardiff and later, in the Second World War, as chief recruiting officer in Northumberland and finally, East Anglia. He retired as a lieut. colonel in 1953 having completed 41 years service.

Captain Willis was 34 years old when he landed at Gallipoli and a veteran of the reconquest of the Sudan where he took part in Battle of Omdurman in 1898. He bore a charmed life on the peninsula until his luck ran out on 4th June during the attack on the Turkish lines in front of Krithia. The battalion suffered over 500 casualties on 'this lamentable day' (in the words of the regimental history) and Willis was wounded by a bullet which lodged beneath his heart. He was evacuated to Egypt and thence to England where he made a full recovery. Promoted to major in September 1915 he was posted to the regiment's 2nd battalion in France. He served on the Somme and in the Ypres salient and finished the war as a lieut. colonel and commandant of a reinforcement camp. Willis returned to his regiment before he retired in November 1920. In later life he worked as a tutor and teacher but the financial rewards of such a career were meagre and he was forced at the age of 81, and with failing eyesight, to advertise that 'he was in desperate need' of a loan of £100. His plight was mentioned in the House of Commons but does not appear to have been followed up with practical help. The sister of a deceased V.C. offered to make the loan. He died in 1966, aged 88.

Cuthbert Bromley was commissioned into the Lancashire Fusiliers in May 1898 and later volun-

Below: Captain R.R.Willis V.C.

teered for the West African Frontier Force. He saw active service in Nigeria and was one of fourteen British Army officers to qualify for the clasp 'Aro 1901-1902' to his Africa General Service Medal. He then returned to his regiment with which he served in India and Ireland. At Gallipoli in 1915, despite injuring his back while landing on W Beach on 25th April, Bromley refused to report sick until he was shot in the knee during the first advance on Krithia three days later. Forced into hospitalisation he returned to the battalion on 17th May as soon as he could hobble.

Promoted to major he was then in temporary command of the battalion which he led at the Battle of Gully Ravine on 28th June. Wounded in the heel early in the advance he refused to seek medical aid but lurched forward using two Turkish rifles as makeshift crutches. He was only persuaded to go to a field dressing station after he had worked throughout the night to ensure that his men's hard earned gains were consolidated.

Evacuated to Egypt he discharged himself from hospital and appears to have wangled a passage on the SS *Royal Edward*, a 11,117 tons liner under charter as a troop transport, which was returning to Gallipoli with reinforcement drafts and recovered wounded. On 13th August 1915, six miles west of Kandeliusa Island in the Mediterranean, she was attacked by a German submarine, the U-15, and torpedoed full on the stern. The transport was fully laden with 31 officers and 1,335 troops, in addition to a crew of 220, and sank very quickly. Thirteen officers and 852 men plus most of the crew were lost, despite the efforts of the hospital ship *Soudan* and two French destroyers which arrived on the scene.

Captain Bromley was among the dead together with 26 recovered wounded from his battalion. These included the oldest man in the unit, No.688 Pte. Bill Cruse, and two men, 5260 Matthew Carroll and 5261 Pat Carney who had joined the regiment on the same day and were fated to die on the same day. All their names appear, with many thousands of others of the dead who have no known graves on the Helles Memorial at Gallipoli.

The last British troops were evacuated from Cape Helles during the night of 8/9th January 1916. By that time the Lancashires, reinforced several times, had lost another 392 other ranks killed and more than double that number wounded. Allied casualties for the entire Dardanelles campaign amounted to 252,000.

11
The Man with a Donkey
Anzac Cove, Gallipoli, April 1915

John Simpson Kirkpatrick was an Englishman who regarded himself as an Australian; certainly he had all the qualities of a devil-may-care Aussie. After leaving his home at South Shields, County Durham, in October 1909, three months after his seventeenth birthday, he spent the next five years mostly as a fireman aboard Australian ships, usually coasters. In between trips there was a stint as a miner in Northern Queensland and several jaunts as a swagman (travelling jack of all trades). As soon as war was declared Kirkpatrick jumped ship in Freemantle and made his way to Perth, where he joined up. There, for reasons of his own, he dropped his surname and enlisted as Private Jack Simpson No.202, Australian Army Medical Corps.

On 25th April 1915, the day of the first landings on the Gallipoli Peninsular, Simpson went ashore on Z Beach with the rest of his section. That night he found a donkey in a deserted hut and thereafter trudged up and down 'Shrapnel Valley' carrying wounded men down to the beach. Although the valley was a dangerous place, exposed to sniper fire in addition to being continually shelled, Simpson continued his one-man rescue service every day and part of each night for three weeks. The man with a donkey, whom he named 'Murphy,' soon became known to everyone from the General downwards. It has been estimated that Simpson and 'Murphy' between them removed over 200 wounded men to safety, but on 19th May luck for both of them ran out. Simpson was buried on a small hill near the sea-shore, known as Queensland Point, now Beach Cemetery, Anzac Cove.

The Australian Official War Historian, C. E. W. Bean, wrote, 'On the night of April 15th he annexed a donkey, and each day, a half of every night, he worked continuously between the head of Monash Valley and the beach, his donkey carrying a brassard round its forehead and a wounded man on its back. Simpson

Above: Z Beach (ANZAC Cove), Gallipoli looking from Fisherman's Hut towards Ari Burnu. Disintegrating ship's boats on beach and Turkish barbed wire in left foreground. Photographed in 1919 (Keith Tranmer).

escaped death so many times that he was completely fatalistic; the deadly sniping down the valley and the most furious shrapnel fire never stopped him. The colonel of his ambulance, recognising the value of his work, allowed him to carry on as a completely separate unit. He camped with his donkey at the Indian mule camp, and had only to report once a day at the field ambulance. Presently he annexed a second donkey. On May 19th he went up the valley... he never came back. With two patients he was coming down the creek bed when he was hit through the heart, both the wounded men being wounded again. He had carried many scores of men down the valley, and had saved many lives at the cost of his own.'

Colonel (later General Sir) John' Monash, commanding the 4th Brigade, in a letter dated 20th May 1915 to ANZAC H.Q., wrote 'I desire to bring under special notice for favour of transmission to the proper authority, the case of Private Simpson, stated to belong to 'C' Section, 3rd Field Ambulance. This man has been working this valley since 26 April, in collecting the wounded, and carrying them to the dressing stations. He had a small donkey which he used to carry all cases unable to walk.' The letter added that Simpson and his donkey were yesterday killed by shrapnel, and enquiry then elicited that he had become separated from his own unit (?) and had carried on his perilous work on his own initiative.

Simpson was recommended for the Victoria Cross but the powers-that-be denied him the award on the grounds that paragraph 5 of the decoration's Warrant referred only to 'some signal act of valour, or devotion to their country.' Apparently acts of valour repeated time and time again did not count, and two decades were to pass before Simpson's outstanding bravery was officially recognised.

Twenty years later a bronze statue of Simpson and his donkey, commissioned by the Red Cross Society, was unveiled in 1935, and stands on the left of the entrance at Melbourne's Shrine of Remembrance. In 1988 Australia's legendary hero received further recognition when a bronze, depicting 'the man with a donkey' was placed on the front of the Australian War Memorial at Canberra. It was a far cry from a humble home in South Shields and a grave on Gallipoli.

12
Canada Holds the Line
10th Canadian Battalion,
Second Ypres, April 1915

The Tenth Canadian Battalion, officially formed in September 1914 was one of the numerous formations raised by Canada as her sons, many of them born in Britain, flocked to the Colours. Not all the men were raw recruits as over half the rank and file had seen previous service in various British regiments or the Royal Navy before emigrating overseas. One of the volunteers, with the imposing names of Royal Alexander Willingham, an English born Texan, displayed a familiarity with military life which occasioned comment among his colleagues that he must have previously served in the U.S. armed forces, or possibly the Texas Rangers. In fact his experience had been gained on the other side of the border whilst serving in the Mexican Army! Attestation papers of the men showed a wide range of pre-war jobs, everything from bank clerks to lumber jacks, but Private Charles Ford's occupation was the most unusual - he described himself as a 'Gentleman Adventurer.' The unit also enlisted a high proportion of brothers, five of these, and four father and son duos but sadly, in the case of George and Peter Cumming and William Walpole and William Walpole junior, the fathers survived the war but the sons, Peter and William junior, were to be killed in action.

On Tuesday 29th September 1914 the Tenth Battalion's 43 officers and 1,051 other ranks embarked on the SS *Scandinavian* at Quebec City docks along with 89 cases of rifles, together with ammunition, stores and 21,109 sacks of flour, the latter a gift from Canada to the mother country. Although the flour was undoubtedly gratefully received the same could not be said of the Canadian manufactured Mark III Ross rifles which were to present grave problems when the men went into action. The ship, which sailed in convoy, entered Plymouth Harbour on 14th October where the Tenth disembarked and moved to Salisbury Plain to spend the next four months training. A major innovation at this time was the formation of a machine-gun section, as each battalion in the Canadian contingent was issued with four American Colt air-cooled, belt fed machine-guns.

Eventually, training completed, amid groundless fears that the war would be over by Christmas, the men were packed like sardines into the *Kingstonian*, an old cattle boat, which crossed the English Channel and arrived at St. Nazaire on 13th February 1915. The arrival was celebrated by the boat running aground on a sandbank, losing two anchors, and bumping up and down on the sand in gale force winds for the next twenty four hours. Finally, at 4 a.m. the next day the aged (and battered) *Kingstonian* floated off the sand-bank and docked soon afterwards. There was a slight hiccup when the Canadians discovered that sitting on the dock, and within easy reach of their hell ship, was an unguarded supply of rum (a sovereign remedy for sea-sickness which was affecting many of the men). British authorities had the temerity to allege that large quantities of the said rum had found its way into Canadian throats, canteens and water bottles. This was strenuously denied but still cost the battalion a fine of 900 francs - about £36 sterling.

Disembarkation began at 7.30 a.m. on 15th February and the Tenth moved inland to spend the next few weeks in various parts of the Front training and undergoing battle indoctrination. On 10th March the battalion manned front line trenches when the British launched their offensive at Neuve Chapelle, adjacent to the Canadian sector. The Canadian assignment was limited to providing artillery and small arms fire to contain the enemy opposite but this diversionary role revealed an alarming problem with the Ross rifles when they were used for rapid fire. After a few rounds rapid the bolt repeatedly jammed after firing a shot and the firer was unable to eject the empty cartridge case by normal manual manipulation of the bolt handle, but was driven to literally hammer open the bolt with the heel of his boot in order to free the sticking case. Not surprisingly the rate of fire fell from fifteen aimed rounds per minute to a figure of two or three, with the result that the men lost confidence in their Canadian made rifles and swapped them at the first opportunity for Lee-Enfields left behind by British casualties. Both weapons chambered a .303 round. In fact the Ross had been extensively tested in Britain between 1900 and 1912 and rejected because it had been designed purely as a target rifle without regard to the effect of dirt, dust and rapid fire under active service conditions. However, the unofficial changeover of rifles was banned and late in March the C.O. ordered all Lee-Enfields to be handed in to Ordnance. It was not until 6th June 1916 that the entire Canadian Division would be issued with the Lee-Enfield, Mark III, but well before that date the battalion would earn for itself the nickname of 'The Fighting Tenth.'

The Canadians now moved north into Belgium for their introduction to the Ypres salient, which was flat, muddy and dangerous. Not only was it invested on three sides by the enemy, but the Germans in this case also occupied what high ground there was near Passchendaele. From this vantage point the Germans, with a superior weight of artillery, could bring down a curtain of fire practically anywhere in the salient which made movement by day in the British lines a perilous adventure. The Canadian sector, about 4,000 yards in length ran from Berlin Wood, 800 yards east of Gravenstafel, to the Ypres-Poelcappelle road which marked the boundary of the French 45th Algerian Division. Trenches which had been vacated by the French were occupied by the Tenth who found that the so-called trenches varied in depth from nothing to two or three feet. A single strand of wire out in front constituted the barbed wire entanglement. But as the French explained - it was a very quiet sector. The dugouts were filthy and the floor of the trench was composed of dead Germans who tended to bubble when they were stepped on. During the Tenth's tenure the defences were improved with over 6,000 sandbags to build up the parapets but nothing could be done about the Germans underfoot. Some days previously a German deserter who had made his way into the French lines reported that an attack was imminent which would be preceded by poison gas. However, as the Germans were signatories to the Hague Convention which banned the use of toxic chemicals in warfare, this rumour was not widely believed.

On 19th April the Tenth's front line tour ended and the battalion marched back to Ypres where it was placed in brigade reserve. Three days later a group of the Tenth's officers were quietly riding their horses along the west bank of the Canal Yser when they heard the noise of a heavy bombardment falling on the French sector, north of the Canadian line. The riders galloped back to their battalion headquarters where they learned that the Tenth would parade at 6 p.m. in full battle order, plus 300 rounds per man, and be ready to move into the battle zone.

Advancing behind clouds of chlorine gas the Germans had attacked and routed the 45th Algerian and the 87th Territorial Divisions holding the northern edge of the salient. When the French Algerian and Turco infantry fled, coughing and retching from the effects of this terrible new weapon, they left behind a gap about 4½ miles wide which exposed the Canadian Division's left flank and endangered the rest of the salient. By early evening the enemy had advanced over 2½ miles and up to the heights known as Mauser Ridge from which they threatened Ypres and St. Julien in the Canadian rear. Fortunately for the Allies there were no German reserves available to exploit the breakthrough and the enemy infantry began to entrench instead of continuing their advance.

Colonel Boyle, C.O. of the Tenth, and his company commanders reported to Brigade H.Q. at Mousetrap Farm which had once been comfortably behind the firing line but was now practically in the front line. Bullets were continually hitting the farm buildings as the General outlined his plan to the assembled officers; instead

Below: 'Canada Holds the Line' - Ypres Salient 22nd April 1915.

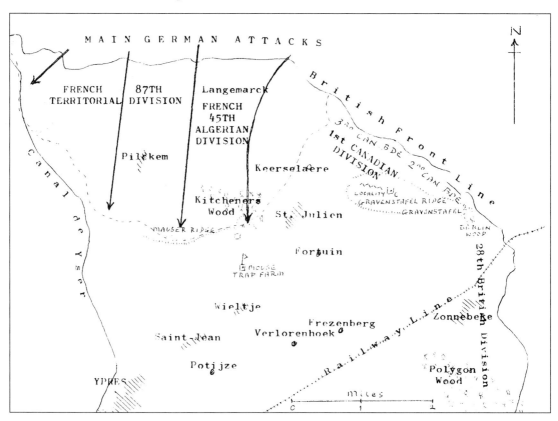

Above: Lt.-Col. R.L.Boyle.

of holding a defensive position the battalion would be used to spearhead a counter-attack. This would be the first major offensive action undertaken by Canadian troops in the Great War and their objective was the capture of a nearby oak plantation, later known as Kitchener's Wood, on the east side of Mauser Ridge. The battalion, 816 strong (200 men had been left behind in reserve), formed up on a 300 yard front with 'A' and 'C' companies in the lead and 'B' and 'D' companies 30 yards behind them in close support, the Canadian 16th battalion, a kilted unit, assembled in similar formation directly in the rear.

At 11.48 p.m. the Canadians advanced and all went well until about 200 yards from the wood when they encountered a hedge, four to six feet high, threaded with barbed wire. Unavoidable noise in breaking through the obstacle alerted the opposition and enemy flares revealing the oncoming troops moving in mass formation. Within seconds a storm of machine-gun and rifle fire swept across the first waves and the rear ranks were soon stumbling over the dead and wounded of their leading files. Despite staggering losses the two battalions, by now completely intermixed, surged across a German trench and into the wood which masked a number of sandbagged machine-gun posts and nearly two battalions of enemy infantry. In the darkness, amid bullet splintered trees, there was savage hand to hand fighting as small groups slugged it out with bombs, bayonets, butts and boots. By midnight it was all over and the Canadians, attacking over unreconnoitred ground with the benefit of only partial surprise, had captured a semi-fortified position held by veteran troops of the 2nd Prussian Guard and 234th Bavarian Infantry Regiment.

Just inside the wood the Canadians discovered four guns of the 2nd London Heavy Brigade which had been taken by the Germans earlier in the day, after a bloody struggle which had cost the lives of the dead British, Turcos and Germans piled high in the gun pits. These guns had to be left for the time being as the first task of the new tenants was the consolidation of their gains. This was made difficult by the fact that insufficient men were on their feet, however widely spaced, to hold the wood

The Canadians had punched over half a mile into enemy-held territory, and with both flanks in the air they were under fire from every direction except south-east. Every company commander had been wounded and Colonel Boyle had fallen with five machine-gun bullets in his groin. Command now devolved on Colonel Leckie, C.O. of the 16th, who ordered the remaining men to fall back and hold the captured German trench on the southern edge of the wood. The four heavy guns were left behind but only after Canadian engineers had wrecked the breech blocks and detonated the stockpiled shells. Also left behind were Captains George Coldwell and Thomas Fryer together with 26 other ranks, all wounded, five of whom died from their injuries before reaching a prisoner of war camp. This was the largest number of men ever taken by the Germans and in fact the battalion only had 35 rank and file captured during the entire war. Twelve men of the Tenth were officially reported as missing after the fighting in the wood but their bodies were never recovered.

A hasty roll call at 6.30 a.m. on the 23rd showed the temporary commanding officer that there was not much left to command. The Tenth had five officers and 188 men still ready for action and the 16th had lost two-thirds of its strength and was left with five officers and 263 rank and file. As well as heavy shelling throughout the day it was impossible for any of the Tenth or 16th to aid the wounded as the slightest movement in the trench also brought deadly fire from enemy snipers and machine-gunners. In addition, the left edge of the trench was under fire from a troublesome German redoubt in the south-western corner of the wood. Here, Lance Corporal Baker and a party of bombers fought a separate battle of their own for nearly twenty four hours, and when supplies of Mills bombs were exhausted the nimble Baker caught German stick grenades in mid-air and returned them to their owners. L/Cpl. Baker, albeit wounded, was the sole survivor of his bombing group and was later awarded a well earned D.C.M. and a French Croix de Guerre avec Palme.

That afternoon a company from the 2nd Battalion was sent to take the 'Baker' redoubt and then reinforce the Tenth/16th survivors in their battered position. The assault failed and not more than ten to 15 men ever reached the Canadian trench. Nightfall brought relief from the incessant shelling and a signaller, working in the open, managed to repair the telephone line to Brigade H.Q. As soon as the line was open requests were made for ammunition, water, rations and stretchers and these were met, with the exception of stretchers; the wounded were obliged to spend another night in the trench.

At about 4 a.m. on Saturday 24th April the enemy opened a ferocious bombardment on the Canadian sector and in the early morning light the defending infantry could see a thick cloud of greenish-yellow gas rolling towards them. Thus dawned what the Canadian Official History records as 'a great and terrible day for Canada.' In an all-out bid to smash the Canadian Division and take the salient the Germans threw 34 battalions against the remains of eight Canadian battalions holding a line between St. Julien and Gravenstafel. This was supported by a five to one superiority in artillery of all calibres. There were no British respirators available at this stage of the war and the defenders tied pieces of cloth, soaked in their own urine or some of their precious water, over their mouths and nostrils to minimise the effects of chlorine gas. At one stage the enemy broke through the 15th Battalion at a point where the gas concentration was heaviest and the 15th was outside the range of its own field guns. This move threatened the entire Canadian position and the Tenth/16th were ordered to withdraw and the Tenth fell back to the 2nd Infantry Brigade H.Q. at Pond Farm.

By this time the battalion was barely the size of a company and mustered three officers and 171 other ranks. Almost immediately the Tenth was ordered back into action to reinforce a company of the 7th Battalion which was holding a vitally important position, known as locality C, on top of Gravenstafel Ridge. En route, under fire all the way, Major Dan Ormond the acting C.O., already slightly wounded, was blown off his feet by a shell burst and soon afterwards fell into a deep water-filled ditch and had to swim for it. It was about this time that he acquired the nickname of 'Dangerous Dan.'

Reaching locality C at about 5.30 a.m. the Tenth moved onto the left of the 7th Battalion men in time to see swarms of Germans led by officers on horseback advancing against their position. Three times the enemy attacked en masse and three times they we beaten back by men who were still kicking at the bolt handles of their Ross rifles in a frenzied effort to maintain at least three aimed rounds per minute. Rank and file of the Tenth now numbered 146 and the position was in the air,

enfiladed from three sides. At 12.15 p.m. the surviving 7th/Tenth men fell back to a road behind the Ridge which gave them a degree of protection. Here Major Ormond was again wounded and handed over command to Captain Arthur, 40 years of age and the oldest man present. Corporal Schultz, the Polish-born medical orderly, made sure that every wounded man was off the Ridge and Private Ross moved through heavy fire on three occasions to bring in wounded men who would otherwise have been left for the Germans. Both men were later awarded a well-deserved D.C.M.

Meanwhile, one of the Tenth's machine-gun crews under L/Cpl. Allan had been loaned to the 2nd Battalion which had reinforced the Tenth/l6th early Friday morning in and around Kitchener's Wood. Allan was ordered to a farmhouse situated in an open field about 75 yards in front of the 2nd's main position, and here the eight crew set up their Colt heavy machine-gun in a ground floor window. The building was a dismal place with all the windows and doors blown out, numerous shell holes in the roof and walls, and one of the rooms was given over to the dead

Above: Locality 'C,' Second Ypres. Cpl. Schultz, 10th Canadian Bn. wins the D.C.M. (*Deeds that Thrill the Empire*).

who were covered in old sacks. Furthermore, the farm's well water was slimy, rank, and virtually undrinkable.

A day-long fire fight then ensued between the defenders comprising the machine-gun crew plus fifteen riflemen against hordes of Germans who made at least six attempts to storm the farm. Between attacks the Colt was manhandled into different positions, including the upper floor and the loft, until it was knocked out and the crew killed or wounded; Allan was one of the wounded. During a brief lull in the battle another crew with a machine-gun managed to gain the building and continue the fight, still commanded by L/Cpl. Allan. Finally, both the weapon and crew were put out of action and Allan fired his rifle until he was hit in the head and killed. Mentioned in despatches and recommended for the Victoria Cross his actual award, unusual in itself, was a posthumous D.C.M.

After dark, at about 9 p.m., the survivors of the 7th/Tenth trudged back to the G.H.Q. line where they were given a hot meal and settled down to sleep. An hour later they were roused, for what was left of the two battalions, about 300 men all told, were urgently needed back at Gravenstafel Ridge. Some time later the composite unit moved into position in a line extending from the Ridge to the Hannebeek, a small stream to the west. At 4 a.m. on Sunday 25th the defenders beat off a dawn assault and both sides began to dig in. No further infantry attacks were made by the enemy but the Canadian troops were hammered by artillery firing at them from two directions, Passchendaele and German occupied St. Julien, and swept by fire from machine-guns sited in a ruined house on the unit's left rear. As casualties mounted it was obvious that the position could not be held but it was not until midnight that the Tenth received an order to retire. The other Canadian and British battalions had been warned at 5 p.m. to withdraw but the runners sent to warn the Tenth had been killed or captured. Thanks to darkness and a heavy mist the Tenth successfully disengaged during the small hours of Monday, 26th April. The men had now been in practically continuous action since midnight on the 22nd.

By dawn on that Monday the four shredded battalions of the 2nd Canadian Infantry Brigade assembled near Wieltje behind the G.H.Q. line, but before they could move back to rest and recuperate the Germans renewed their infantry attacks on the British units which had relieved the Canadian Division. A report (later found to be false) that the enemy had broken through sent the dog tired Canadians back towards Gravenstafel Ridge. There the men were deployed in open fields near Fortuin where they were heavily shelled throughout the day. Finally, in the early hours of Tuesday, 27th April the brigade moved out and marched back to Ypres. The Fighting Tenth now numbered 98 all ranks, including the walking wounded.

Despite the battalion's outstanding combat record very few decorations were handed out, probably because most of the officers who could have made the recommendations were killed or in hospital wounded. Colonel Boyle, who died from his wounds, was mentioned in despatches; 'Dangerous Dan' received the Russian Order of St. Stanislas, third class with swords; and Captain Arthur who had briefly commanded the Tenth, despite being wounded was awarded the D.S.O. Six of the rank and file received the D.C.M.

Above: Impressive head and shoulders of a Canadian soldier resting on his arms reversed, surmounting the pillar of the Canadian Memorial at Vancouver Corner, one km from St Julien (J. Rooke-Matthews).

The Tenth was reformed, in fact it would be reformed many times during the next three years owing to a casualty list which named 165 officers and 4,391 other ranks killed, wounded or gassed. By the end of the war members of the battalion had been awarded a staggering total of 493 decorations, ranging from two Victoria Crosses to 88 mentions in despatches. 'Dangerous Dan' finished the war as a brigadier general, a Companion of the Order of St. Michael and St. George with the D.S.O. and bar, and a French Croix de Guerre to add to his Russian order. He stayed in the army and retired as a major general in 1932.

After the war, on 6th December 1918, the Fighting Tenth marched into Germany for a brief spell in the Army of Occupation before the battalion moved to England and thence to Canada, landing at Halifax on Good Friday, 18th April 1919 to be demobilised. The veterans of Gravenstafel and St. Julien were few and far between.

13
A Man Named Jacka
14th Battalion A.I.F., Gallipoli, May 1915

By the middle of May 1915, three weeks after the initial landing on Z Beach, (officially renamed 'Anzac Cove' three days later) the Australians were still clinging to their beach-head. Clinging was the operative word because the Turks held most of the crest of the ridges overlooking the beach, and the invaders could only just hold on to the bullet-swept approach slopes. In places the opposing trenches were only five to ten yards apart.

At 3.30 a.m. on 19th May, the Turks launched a massive attack, deploying some 40,000 troops against the Anzac perimeter, in an all-out effort to push the Aussies back down onto the beach and into the sea. But as the enemy came over the crest they were met by a storm of fire and only in one place did they manage to penetrate the defences. At this point however, before they could exploit their success, they were killed or beaten back by one man, Acting Lance Corporal Jacka of the 14th Battalion, Australian Imperial Force.

On the morning of the attack, the 14th's sector included Courtney's Post, which was centred between Quinn's Post to the north and Stelle's Post on the south, and these three posts held a vital position at the head of a gully which bisected the entire Anzac beach-head. Courtney's took its name from the C.O. of the 14th whose men held that part of the 4th Australian Infantry Brigade line. At the time of the assault A/L/Cpl. Jacka with about ten men of his platoon from 'D' Company was manning a section of trench on the left of the position when a party of Turks took advantage of some dead ground in front of Courtney's to creep to within a few feet of the parapet. From this vantage point they bombed the Anzac trench, killing two defenders and wounding two more, and causing the remainder to abandon the position. This left the Turks occupying some 12 vital yards of trench at the head of Monash Valley. Unbeknown to them, however, one man, Albert Jacka, was still holding his ground behind a traverse in the next-door bay.

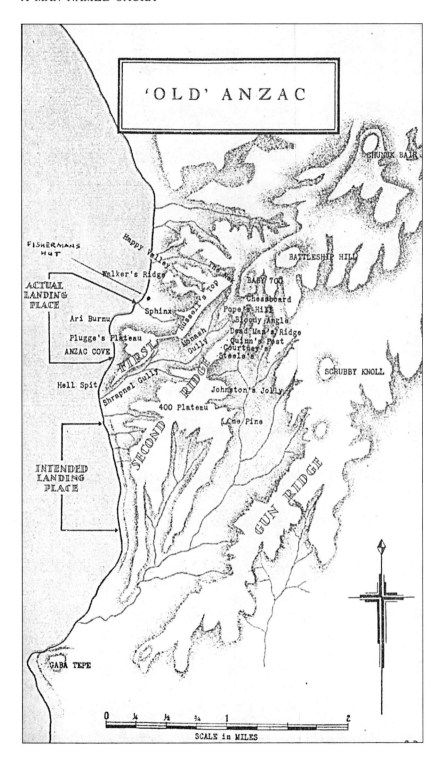

'OLD' ANZAC

Jacka's first reinforcement was a subaltern from his own company armed only with a revolver, who tried to dislodge the enemy by charging along the communications trench; he was shot dead. Then for a period of about 15 minutes Jacka remained the only obstacle to the Turks breaking out to the north. He was eventually joined by Lieut. Crabbe and four volunteers, but their first attempt to overcome the enemy failed when two of the group were shot. Jacka and Crabbe now hatched a second and near suicidal plan which would involve Jacka climbing out into No-Man's-Land, which was still the scene of furious fighting, and falling upon the enemy from the rear.

As Jacka set off, the party's only two bombs were hurled towards the enemy's fire bay and the riflemen fired into the wall of the bay in an effort to convince the intruders that they were about to be attacked from the north. Meanwhile, Jacka ran the length of the communications trench, ducked in behind the firebay, and climbed out into No-Man's-Land. Then, with the Turks still distracted, Jacka leapt in among them. The story of the ensuing struggle has been told many times and details tend to vary but, according to the 14th's historian, Jacka bayoneted two Turks, shot five, and killed two more as they fled over the parapet. Yet another source states that he also took three prisoners. It is not known how many of the enemy had occupied the trench but certainly two wounded Turks and 26 Turkish rifles were recovered from the body-strewn bay. By now the enemy attack had failed all along the line and, according to the Turkish official account, their losses amounted to ten thousand and more than three thousand dead were counted that afternoon in front of the Australian trenches.

Jacka was ill in hospital on the island of Imbros when the award of his Victoria Cross was announced in the *London Gazette* of 24th July 1915. The citation read; 'For most conspicuous bravery on the night of the 19th-20th May 1915 at Courtney's Post, Gallipoli Peninsula. Lance-Corporal Jacka, while holding a portion of our trench with four other men, was heavily attacked. When all except himself were killed or wounded, the trench was rushed and occupied by seven Turks. Lance-Corporal Jacka at once most gallantly attacked them single-handed, and killed the whole party, five by rifle-fire and two with the bayonet.' This account, in common with other V.C. citations, seems to contain more than its fair share of errors.

From a lance corporal in May to full corporal in August, sergeant on 12th September and C.S.M. by November, rapid promotion came to Jacka after the award of his Cross. Commissioned a second lieutenant on 29th April 1916 he accompanied his battalion to France where he was again in the forefront of the action.

Early on the morning of 7th August 1916, during the Battle of Pozières, Jacka's platoon was isolated by an enemy onslaught which smashed through the front line on both his flanks. A grenade thrown into his dugout killed two of the occupants and wounded Jacka just before he led a remarkable counter-attack. The victorious German infantry obviously thought their part in the action was over and they were busy rounding up about 40 prisoners from a neighbouring Australian unit when suddenly Jacka followed by seven men was among them, shooting and bayoneting. His battalion's history states, 'Jacka, hurled off his feet on different occasions by the terrific impact of rifle bullets fired at close range, was seven times wounded, once being knocked down by a bullet that passed through his body under the right shoulder, and twice partially stunned by head wounds. He fairly surpassed himself this day, and killed upwards of a score of Germans with his own hand, including some with the bayonet... all the Australian prisoners were released, the whole

Below: Captain Albert Jacka V.C. (left) congratulating Pte. O'Meara of the 15th A.I.F. after he had won the V.C. at Pozières in 1916.

of the German escort guarding them was killed or dispersed, and in addition 42 unwounded Germans were captured.' His audacity on this occasion earned him a Military Cross.

Convalescent in England, Jacka was promoted lieutenant on 18th August and reported dead on 8th September but, very much alive despite his wounds, he received his V.C. at Windsor Castle on 29th September. In due course he returned to the Western Front where he was promoted to captain on 15th March 1917. The following month, while serving as battalion intelligence officer, he made a number of dangerous patrols in No-Man's-Land including a daring reconnaissance of the German front line on the eve of the Battle of Bullecourt. On this last occasion he captured a German two-man patrol single-handed and earned a bar to his M.C.

During the battle for Messines Ridge in June 1917, Jacka led his company in an advance which overran three machine-gun posts and captured a German field gun but, although two of his men were decorated, Jacka's own actions passed unrecognised. Later, after recovering from yet another wound, he distinguished himself during the fighting near Polygon Wood when the 14th captured and held its ground against heavy and determined German counter-attacks. On this occasion he was recommended for a D.S.O., which never materialised. He sustained further severe injuries in May 1918 but following two operations and a long convalescence he recovered and returned home to a hero's welcome in September 1919.

In 1930 Jacka became mayor of St. Kilda, Australia, but he collapsed at a council meeting in December 1931 and died in Caulfield Military Hospital of chronic nephritis on 17th January 1932. Although he was only 39 years of age he looked very much older and his many war wounds had finally taken their toll. After his death C.E.W. Bean, the Australian Official War Historian wrote, 'Jacka should have come out of the war the most decorated man in the AIF... Everyone who knows the facts, knows that Jacka earned the Victoria Cross three times.' This view was shared by one of Jacka's contemporaries who had served with him in the 14th. 'His leadership in his last battle was as audacious and capable as in his first. He deserved the Victoria Cross as thoroughly at Pozières, Bullecourt and Ypres as at Gallipoli. Not we only, but the brigade, and the whole AIF came to look upon him as a rock of strength that never failed.'

Extraordinary tributes to an extraordinary man.

14

An Officer and a Gentleman
– and a Deserter?

2nd Queen's (Royal West Surrey) Regiment, Battle of Festubert, May 1915

At 2.45 a.m. on 16th May 1915 British artillery began to shell German positions east of Festubert in order to soften up the defenders as a preliminary to an infantry attack. Unfortunately, owing to a shortage of heavy calibre ammunition the bombardment was limited to 30 minutes duration and, even more unfortunately many of the shells dropped short into the British lines causing a number of casualties. When the troops went over the top the most successful attack was made against the enemy in their Rue d'Overt trenches where the 1st Battalion, Royal Welch Fusiliers with the 2nd Queen's (Royal West Surrey) Regiment on their right, despite heavy losses crossing No-Man's-Land, took the first line of German trenches. Here, however, success wavered in the balance with hand to hand fighting against a numerically superior enemy in the tangled system of interlocking trenches. The outcome now depended on a handful of men maintaining a foothold until the reserves could reach them.

At this point C.S.M. Frederick Barter of 'C' Company of the R.W.F., the senior rank left alive in the company, called for volunteer bombers and collected eight, including one from the Queen's. With his eight volunteers Barter steadily bombed his way from left to right clearing five hundred yards of trenches and capturing three officers and 102 men. He also found the time to cut eleven mine leads which would have negated the attack had they been detonated. The eighth soldier whom the regimental history mentions as 'a Queen's man' was Private Thomas Hardy who had been temporarily attached to the Royal Welch for training as a bomber. During the battle in the trenches Hardy was hit by a bullet in the right shoulder and Barter shouted at him to retire. Hardy replied that his injury did not matter as he was left handed and continued bombing until he was shot in the head and killed. He had been in the forefront of the bombing party with Barter and would

Above: Captain Hugh Sale Smart, 53rd Sikhs, dressed as Pte. Thomas Hardy, Queen's (Royal West Surrey) Regt.

certainly have been recommended for a decoration had he lived.

However, things are sometimes not what they seem, especially in wartime, and Thomas Hardy's real name was Hugh Sale Smart and he was the son of a colonel. On the outbreak of war Smart had been a captain in the 53rd Sikhs (Frontier Force) and on secondment to the Kyber Rifles with whom he had seen active service on the North West Frontier of India in 1908. In 1914 Smart's application to rejoin his own unit, the 53rd Sikhs, which was under orders for overseas service, was refused. Determined to take an active part in the fighting, Smart made his own way from India to England and elected to join a British regiment as a private to make sure of getting to the Front and into action. Presumably at that stage he was technically a deserter. When his true identity came to light after his death, he was posthumously reinstated in his previous rank in recognition of his gallantry at Festubert

C.S.M. Barter was awarded the Victoria Cross for his bombing exploit and gained a regular commission. He survived the war and retired as a major.

15

Ordeal by Fire

The 8th (Service) Battalion, Rifle Brigade, Hooge, 30 July 1915

The 7th and 8th Battalions of the Rifle Brigade together with the 7th and 8th Battalions King's Royal Rifle Corps formed the 41st (Green Jackets) Brigade of the 14th (Light) Division which landed in France on 20 May 1915. After the usual period of trench inoculation this formation moved onto the ground assigned, some miles east of Ypres, and relieved the 3rd Division late in July. For some reason which has never been satisfactorily explained the outgoing Division exploded a mine of such dimensions that it left a chasm about 50 yards wide (dubbed the Hooge crater) in the centre of the British front line trench. By way of reply the enemy heavy minenwerfers steadily bombarded the crater and the Germans also exploded their own mine on the western edge of the chasm which destroyed all the work which had been done to repair the ravages caused by enemy trench mortar bombs. Thus the lips of the crater could not be garrisoned and this was to have serious consequences.

At 10 p.m. on 29 July 1915 the 8th Rifle Brigade moved out of Ypres to relieve its sister battalion, the 7th R.B., in the trenches at Hooge and by 2 a.m. on the 30th the take over had been completed. Dispositions of the incoming battalion were as follows: The left of 'C' Company rested on the eastern edge of the crater and its right on the Menin road where it joined the 7th K.R.R.C. which was also in the front line. At this point a communication trench named 'Strand' ran south to the edge of Zouave Wood. No.2 Platoon of 'A' Company manned the portion of trench which turned south to the second line. The remaining part of the battalion's frontage was held by 'A' Company's No.4 Platoon commanded by 2/Lieut. Sydney Woodroffe. Numbers 1 and 3 Platoons of 'A' Company held the second line trench south of the ruins of Hooge. A communication trench, 'Bond Street', ran from this position to the support trench holding 'B' Company on the northern edge of

Zouave Wood. 'D' Company manned the trenches to the right of 'C', also in the wood.

The battalion's war record mentions that it was a dark night with the moon in the 3rd Quarter. It also notes several disturbing points about the position: 1. Very little defensive wire. 2. The front line trenches were deep and narrow and movement along them was extremely difficult. 3. Communication to the rear (i.e. Brigade H.Q.) was difficult. 4. Not only was it impossible to hold the lips of the crater but minenwerfer bombs daily blew in parts of the support trenches rendering them unusable; hence there were too many men crammed into the front line. Furthermore, the usual practice of sending in one company, together with the machine guns and bombers, some hours in advance of the main body had not been followed. Thus all ranks of the 8th were total strangers to the ground and the trenches - where in places the opposing front lines were only 15 yards apart.

At 3.15 a.m. the Germans attacked and parts of the British front line trenches were engulfed in sheets of flame and thick black smoke. Witnesses who were on the flanks of the liquid fire spoke of the intense heat generated by the flames. The new

Right: Hooge, 30th July 1915

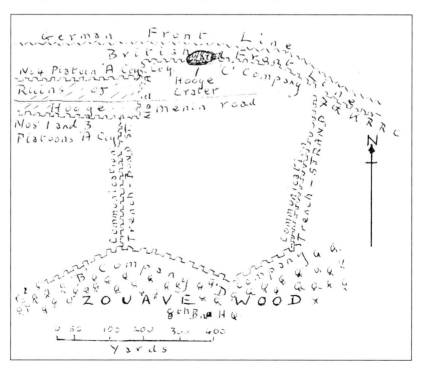

horror weapon had apparently been projected from static pipes protruding through the enemy parapet which the Germans had placed in position during the British changeover. Screams of burned and blinded men were drowned by the noise of exploding bombs fired from heavy calibre minen-werfers in a short but intensive bombardment. This was followed by swarms of enemy bombers, most of whom had broken through at Hooge crater, who were seen fanning out in each direction along the British front line. Only the extreme right and left hand Rifle Brigade platoons in the firing line, who had not been touched by the fire, were able to repulse attempts to bomb them out. In particular, 2/Lieut. Woodroffe and his platoon, cut off from the remainder of the battalion and surrounded by German troops, held off all their supply of bombs was exhausted. Woodroffe then extricated his men in good order and turned about, intending to take the enemy in the flank, but whilst cutting our own wire he was shot down and killed. His bravery earned him a posthumous V.C., the first such award to 'Kitchener's Mob.'

Above: 2/Lt. Sydney Clayton Woodroffe V.C.

But at this stage the British centre had collapsed. Four out of the battalion's five machine-guns had been captured or disabled and the enemy was through Hooge, across the Menin road, and advancing on Zouave Wood almost before news of the disaster had reached the support companies. In addition, German support troops had speedily converted the ruins of Hooge into a whole series of machine-gun nests. Hence when 'B' Company moved out from Zouave Wood the intended counter attack broke down in the face of murderous enemy machine-gun fire. However, the survivors managed to establish themselves in 'Bond Street' and were able to cover the withdrawal of the remnants of 'A' Company. The Germans then attempted to bomb their way down the two communication trenches but these were blocked about half way up and held throughout the day. Meanwhile Zouave Wood had been subjected to a continuing violent artillery bombardment and all telephone wires to brigade had been cut.

Eventually runners got through to higher authority and at 9 a.m. the first reinforcements arrived in the shape of one K.R.R.C. company. About 12 noon orders were received from Division that the 8th, advancing from Zouave Wood with the 9th K.R.R.C. on their right, were to counter-attack and retake Hooge and the neighbouring trenches. The advance would be supported by two battalions of the Rifle Brigade, the 9th and the dog tired 7th who had reached their rest camp at 3.45 a.m. and were roused from sleep an hour later. They eventually reached Zouave Wood at 1.30 p.m.

A 45 minute bombardment would precede the counter-attack which was timed for 2.45 p.m. The decision to launch an attack in daylight was taken against the advice of the Brigadier on the spot. 'In my opinion.' he wired to the divisional commander, 'situation precludes counter-attack by day. Counter-attack would be into a re-entrant and would not succeed in face of enfilade fire.' Division overruled his objection insisting that if no counter-attack were made the Zouave Wood position might become untenable.

Only one untouched company, 'D,' remained in hand; 'C' was non-existent and both 'A' and 'B' had sustained heavy losses. 'D' Company was to attack on a front of two platoons with two platoons in support with its right flank resting on the 'Strand' whilst at the same time bombing up the 'Strand.' The company was to move into position during the shelling and get beyond our own wire which protected the northern edge of Zouave Wood. Remnants of 'A' and 'B' were given practically the same orders but with their centre on 'Bond Street' and to bomb up the communication trench itself. 7th R.B. would act as support to the 8th.

At 2.45 p.m. precisely the counter-attack began but the enemy machine-gunners and riflemen had not been silenced in any way by the British shelling. The Brigadier later reported that the British shells were 'too much distributed and too far forward.' In the event the advance, across ground literally swept by bullets, was brought to a standstill about half way to the objectives. The second counter-attack had failed. To quote the regimental history, 'The attack, like almost every hastily impro-vised operation undertaken by either side during the whole war, was pre-doomed to failure. The utilization, in the forefront, of a spent battalion that on top of the heavy fatigue of a relief and been fighting throughout the remainder of the night, had obtained no rest, and had been without food and water since coming into the line was, to speak mildly, a serious error of judgement...'

The 8th was relieved at 2 a.m. on the 31st and taken out of action. It had lost 63% of its rank and file - 342 men killed and wounded, five shell shocked and 132 missing (missing in this case being synonymous with burned to death). The battalion's officers fared even worse losing 19 out of 24; six killed, three missing and ten wounded. The 7th battalion had lost 16 officers and 300 men.

One of the 8th Battalion officers, Leslie Woodroffe, a former Shrewsbury schoolmaster, was among the severely wounded at Hooge and mentioned in despatches. He recovered from his injuries and returned to the front where he earned the M.C. but was again badly wounded and died of his wounds on 4 June 1916. The Victoria Cross awarded to his brother, Sydney Clayton Woodroffe, was gazetted on 6 September 1915 and the citation read, 'For conspicuous bravery on 30th July, 1915, at Hooge. The enemy having broken through the

Below: Three young officers of 'A' Coy. 8th Rifle Brigade, Lts. Michael Scrimgeour, G.V.Carey and L.A.McAfee. Two would be killed and one wounded at Hooge not long after this photograph was taken.

centre of our front line trenches, consequent on the use of burning liquids, this officer's position was heavily attacked with bombs from the flank and subsequently from the rear, but he managed to defend his post until all his bombs were exhausted and then skilfully withdrew his remaining men. This very gallant officer immediately led his party forward in a counter-attack under an intense rifle and machine-gun fire and was killed whilst in the act of cutting the wire obstacles in the open.'

He has no known grave and his name is commemorated, with many thousands of others, on the Ypres (Menin Gate) Memorial in Belgium. A third Woodroffe brother, Kenneth Herbert, a noted pre-war bowler of county class, had already been killed in action on 9th May 1915 while serving with the 3rd Battalion, Rifle Brigade.

The 8th Battalion, Rifle Brigade, was again severely punished at the Battle of Flers-Courcelette on 15th September 1916 where, at one stage, it was reduced to one unwounded officer and 160 rank and file. Sadly, the battalion was not to retain its identity until the Armistice. It was reduced to a cadre on 27th April 1918 and disbanded on 3rd August 1918.

16
First Territorials into Action
1st London Scottish, Battle of Loos, 25th September 1915

Shortly before the 1st Battalion the 14th (County of London) Regiment, better known as the London Scottish, embarked for France on 15th September 1914 the unit was congratulated by the President of the Territorial Force Association on the 'high honour' of being the first Territorial unit to go to the Front. Six weeks later, fighting for their lives at Messines, no doubt the men would willingly have swapped the 'high honour' for some decent rifles.

At about 10 a.m. on Saturday 31st October 1914, Halloween and dear to the Scots, the battalion, less half a company, moved onto the Messines-Wytschaete ridge in order to reinforce British troops struggling to hold their position against heavy odds. The London Scottish were shelled throughout the day until at 9 p.m. the Germans launched another infantry attack on the ridge. It was a fine night with a full moon and masses of the enemy could be clearly seen cheering as they advanced, with their bands playing in the distance.

When the defenders in their Hodden grey kilts took aim on this splendid close range target a serious defect in their new rifles became apparent. These had been issued only the day before the battalion left England and since landing in France there had been no opportunity for rifle practice. As a result not one man in the unit had ever fired a shot from his new rifle; a Mark I Lee Enfield converted to take Mark VII ammunition. It was not until the London Scottish were in action that they discovered that not only was the magazine spring too weak to lift the next round into position but, even worse, the front stop clips on the magazine were the wrong shape for a Mark VII bullet. So, either the point of the cartridge struck against the lower part of the breech and jammed, or jumped out of alignment and hit the top of the breech chamber, sometimes breaking off the nose of the bullet. Hence, the magazines were useless and the rifles could only be used as single-loaders, with each round manually pushed into the breech before closing the bolt.

Despite being without machine-guns and fighting a modern war with the equivalent of Zulu War weapons the London Scottish managed to beat off three more mass attacks until 2 a.m. when the enemy finally broke through onto the ridge. In the confused fighting the medical officer, Captain MacNab, was bayoneted by a Bavarian soldier while he was attending to a wounded man.

Below: A London Scot of 1914.

With both flanks open the 14th was obliged to retire but fortunately the Germans were too exhausted to interfere with the withdrawal. Indeed they apparently used the lull in the fighting to rally their intermixed units and remove their wounded, and those of the London Scottish, who lay scattered all over the battlefield. A roll call later that morning established that nine officers and 385 other ranks had been killed, or wounded and captured. No. 2148 Private Ronald Colman, 24 years old and formerly a clerk in the City of London, had been one of the earliest casualties when he was badly wounded in the leg; his war had lasted barely an hour. Discharged as medically unfit in February 1915 he always remembered, and often spoke of, his service with the London Scottish even when in the 1930's he became a famous Hollywood film star.

After Messines the 14th was attached to the 1st Guards Brigade near Gheluvelt where it helped to beat off repeated attacks by Prussian Guard regiments. In this engagement a number of the London Scottish were armed with Lee Enfields handed over by the wounded of other units; the remainder, rather than struggle with their single-shot breech loaders, used Mauser rifles and ammunition taken from German dead. Casualties mounted and by 12th November 1914 the unit could only muster 280 all ranks compared with a war strength of 1,007 six weeks earlier. Reinforced by 200 officers and men from the 2nd battalion the 14th were again in action at Givenchy in December 1914, and Neuve Chapelle three months later.

On 15th September 1915 the London Scottish celebrated the anniversary of their arrival in France. This was also the date originally set for the big push when six British divisions, preceded by a massive artillery bombardment and a heavy concentration of gas, would attack on a seven-mile front between Loos and La Bassée. The planners were confident that any Germans in the front line system who survived the shelling would be exterminated by the gas that followed. Hence, the attacking force would suffer few casualties and would be intact when it met the enemy reserves. In addition, masses of cavalry were in readiness behind the line ready to sweep forward and exploit the victory. However, the date of the assault was put back until the 25th to allow additional gas cylinders to be positioned. Amid all these preparations only one thing was missing - the element of surprise. Boards were hoisted over the German front line enquiring in English why the big attack had been postponed!

Reinforced for the forthcoming battle, although these newcomers barely replaced the number of N.C.O.s and men commissioned into other regiments, the London Scottish and the 9th King's Liverpools formed a formation titled 'Green's Force.' Orders for this group were, (a) to move into the British front line as soon as the assaulting 1st and 2nd Infantry Brigades had gone over the top; (b) when those brigades had cleared the German first-line trenches to move forward into the gap and occupy the enemy's reserve line, and (c) maintain connection between the two brigades (whose lines of advance would diverge as they progressed). Finally, and if necessary, Green's Force would assist 1st Brigade in the capture of Hulluch.

At 5.30 a.m. on the 25th British artillery opened up along the line plastering the German front with shells of all calibres. It was a dull rainy day with virtually no wind and the gas released from the British trenches lingered over No-Man's-Land or drifted back into the British positions. Little, if any, of the gas appears to have rolled up the slope and into the German lines. The assaulting infantry left their trenches at 7.30 a.m. and initially all went well; Loos was stormed and the 15th Division went on to attack the infamous Hill 70. On the 1st Division front

1st Infantry Brigade took the first German line and pressed on towards Hulluch, but the 2nd Brigade on its right was soon in trouble. Moving through their own poisonous gas cloud the men found themselves up against great belts of uncut barbed wire and soon became stationary targets for enemy artillery and machine-guns.

Green's Force was ordered to move into the vacated British front line at 8 a.m., but the 2nd Brigade's attack having failed and the covering smoke dispersed, the advance was made in full view of the enemy and the group suffered accordingly. The London Scottish were unable to enter the trenches as they were full of gas and the men were obliged to seek what cover they could behind the low parapets. Away to the left front, men of the 1st Brigade were visible in the German lines but all that could be seen of 2nd Brigade were dead and wounded lying by the German wire and gassed and injured men straggling back towards the British line. It was late afternoon when Green's Force managed to reach the German reserve line by which time casualties from shelling and small arms fire had reduced the group's effectives to about 400.

That evening the London Scottish were attached to 2nd Infantry Brigade and moved to the chalk pit over a mile east of

Right: London Territorials at Loos.

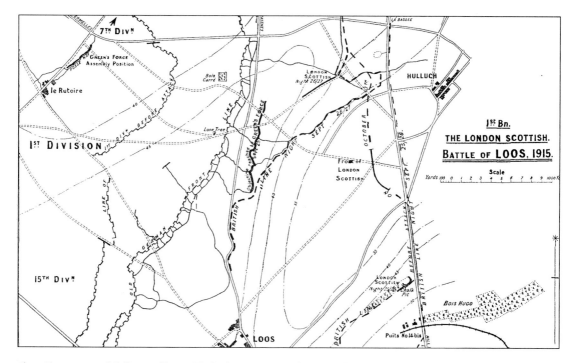

Above: London Scottish at Loos

the German old front line. Unbeknown to the tired and dazed survivors, especially of the 2nd Brigade, the first day of the Battle of Loos had been an overwhelming victory for the British Army. All the objectives had been taken, admittedly at an enormous cost in lives, and it only remained for fresh troops to exploit the situation. But there were no fresh troops. Only the men of the recently formed 21st and 24th Divisions, untried in battle, were pushed into the line after a long and exhausting march. During the forced march they had suffered heavily from shell fire which had also destroyed the divisional transports carrying spare ammunition and rations. Even their water bottles were empty.

The London Scottish were withdrawn to the captured German trenches where they waited, under fire, for fresh orders. In the event they received three sets of orders, all of them contradictory. The bright light of victory was fading and that day (the 26th) the untried Divisions, thrown into action under hopeless conditions were not holding their ground. German troops were winning back some of their lost territory, including the Hohenzollern Redoubt, taken at such cost on the 25th.

On the evening of the 27th another unit relieved the 14th which was withdrawn to the Fosse Way trenches near Le

Rutoire where the London Scottish spent two days chilled to the bone in never-ending rain. Just behind the trench, and with the gun muzzles almost projecting over it, British heavy artillery was in action and attracting counter-battery fire from the enemy. Even sleep was impossible for occupants of the trench due to the noise. During the following evening the battalion was relieved and marched to Moeux-les-Mines where it received yet another batch of reinforcements. This brought the strength of all ranks to about 300, poor compensation for the five officers and 260 men lost in the last engagement.

On October 5th the London Scottish, once more part of the 1st Infantry Brigade, 1st Division, moved back into the line where the Division was to hold a front from Loos Chalk Pit to the Vermelles-Hulluch road. The 14th was the right-hand unit of the brigade and the trenches they occupied were under German artillery fire from the front, and both flanks. On the afternoon of the 7th, after a tremendous bombardment, the enemy attacked in force but was repulsed. In the midst of this action the London Scottish C.O., Colonel Lindsey, was called to Brigade headquarters where he was informed that the brigade would attack the German newly established line on the 11th. The brigade's objective was to be limited to the enemy firing and support trenches. As it was doubtful if the British artillery would be able to cut the German wire, the assaulting troops would have to do that themselves under cover of smoke. Smoke bombs would be thrown into No-Man's-Land one hour before the attacking infantry left their jumping off trenches. Furthermore, no reserves would be available as all five battalions of the brigade were to be committed. Gas was to be used, but not on the 14th's frontage, and the operation was delayed until the 13th October to enable extra gas cylinders to be installed.

As far as the London Scottish were concerned, the first wave would be 'D' Company whose men would carry all the available wire-cutters, with 'A' Company in close support ready to move through the gaps in the wire and take the first enemy trench. 'B' Company would remain in the British firing line until 'A' Company had secured its objective and then leap frog through 'A' to capture the second trench. 'C' Company would stay back in reserve in case of a counter-attack.

The 13th was a dull day with a light wind from the southwest. Zero hour was fixed for 2 p.m. and punctually at 1 p.m. the forward troops began to throw their smoke bombs. However, by 2 p.m. with the wind driving the smoke to the north-east, the smoke screen in front of the London Scottish had all but disappeared. The first two companies gallantly advanced as far as the uncut wire by which time most of the platoon and section commanders, plus the men carrying wire-cutters, had been hit. There was nothing else for the survivors to do but form a firing line in the open and hope that one of the other battalions would have better fortune. It was not to be and by 4.30 p.m. it was obvious that the attack had stalled all along the line. At midnight the London Scottish were relieved by the Civil Service Rifles and next morning, under cover of a thick mist, withdrew to the pre-Loos British line.

In this suicidal action most of the N.C.O.s were casualties as were the five officers who had joined the battalion with drafts since 25th September. Only about 200 other ranks survived, some of them wounded, while 'D' Company, the first wave, had ceased to exist. The battalion had also lost a most unusual man in Private Ford, killed while working as a stretcher bearer in No-Man's-Land. Ford was a former officer of the regiment who resigned his commission in 1903 to take Holy Orders but joined up again as an ordinary private soldier on the outbreak of war.

One of the difficulties which beset the London Scottish was caused by the powers-that-be who treated the battalion as a fighting unit while, at the same time, commissioning some of their best N.C.O.s and men and transferring them elsewhere. Some 6,000 men, mostly from the 1st battalion, had been moved to other regiments in this manner by the end of the war.

The casualty rolls for the 1st battalion remained open long after the tragedy of Loos. On 1st July 1916, the first day of the Somme, the London Scottish suffered 558 casualties all ranks - about 70% of the strength.

17

The Devil's Wood

8th Black Watch, Battle of Delville Wood, 15th July 1916

Delville Wood on the Somme, better known as Devil's Wood to the P.B.I., features in many regimental histories including that of the 8th (Service) Battalion, The Black Watch. Raised in August 1914 this unit, together with the 7th Seaforths, 8th Gordon Highlanders and the 5th Camerons formed the 26th Infantry Brigade, later the 26th (Highland) Brigade of the 9th (Scottish) Division the senior division of Kitchener's New Armies.

The battalion was at war strength, 29 officers and 1,007 other ranks, when it landed in France on 10th May 1915 and moved into the line for an introduction to trench warfare. During the next two years ten of the original 17 subalterns were destined to die in action and another four would be wounded. On 21st September 1915 a four days bombardment signalled the prelude to the Battle of Loos and the first major action for officers and men of the Highland Brigade. The sector allotted to the Scottish Division included the infamous Hohenzollern Redoubt, a strongly held salient which gave the Germans excellent observation over No-Man's-Land to both north and south. Behind this redoubt lay a large slag heap and a coal pit, Fosse No. 8, with a mining village, strangely named in two halves, Corons de Maroc and Corons de Pekin to the north-east.

For the first time in history the British Army used gas, but the weapon was shrouded in great secrecy and always referred to in Divisional orders as 'the accessory.' At 6.30 a.m. on the 25th after a final burst of artillery and machine-gun fire, British troops went over the top on a seven mile front. In the Scots sector Hohenzollern Redoubt and Little Willie Trench (running northwards from the redoubt) had been taken by 7 a.m. and the 8th together with the Camerons pressed on and captured Dump Trench, the main enemy position in front of Fosse No.8.

However, these successes were not gained without heavy casualties among the attackers. The 28th Brigade on the left had been stopped short by uncut wire across its front and this exposed the left flank of the Scots, allowing the Black Watch and the Camerons to be hammered by close range machine-gun fire from Madagascar and Madagascar Point on their left. The Black Watch C.O., Colonel Lord Semphill, was badly wounded near Fosse No.8., Captain Mowbray of 'B' Company was killed and the other two company commanders, Major Henderson 'A' and Major Stewart 'C' were both wounded. Three subalterns had been killed and all but four of the other officers wounded.

From Dump Trench the advance continued and by 9.30 a.m. Corons de Pekin and the Fosse were held by an intermixed force of Black Watch and Camerons. Command of the battalion now devolved on Major Collins who deployed the remaining men on a line along the eastern face of Corons de Pekin. At about 6 p.m. information was received that the brigade on the right had fallen back and as the left flank was already exposed this meant that both flanks were in the air. Despite this the Highlanders held their ground although there were only three Lewis Guns still in action with very few drums of ammunition to feed them. In addition, two of the four Vickers had been knocked out, one lost at Railway Well and the other, under Sgt. Anderson who was killed together with his team, had been destroyed near Haisnes while engaging a German battery at close range.

About midnight the survivors of the Highland Brigade were relieved by men from the 24th Division who had just arrived in France and were rushed straight into the line after a long and tiring march. Before the changeover had been completed the enemy launched a counter-attack, but it was finally beaten off and the Scots were able to withdraw to the old front line where they remained in reserve for 24 hours. At dawn on the 27th men from the relieving force were seen falling back amid a shower of German bombs and it was obvious that Fosse No.8 had been lost and the enemy was rapidly regaining the Redoubt. A force of 70 men from the Black Watch and 30 Cameron Highlanders under Capt. Fergus Bowes-Lyon were ordered to make for the Redoubt and rally any men seen retiring, but during the fight Bowes-Lyon and his subaltern, Lieut. MacIntosh, were both killed. The present Queen Mother still mourns her brother Fergus even after a period of eighty years. He has no known grave and his name is commemorated on Loos Memorial.

Eventually the position was stabilised but not before Major Collins and R.S.M. Black were also slain. The battalion was then commanded by the senior surviving officer, Capt. Ewing, the adjutant. On September 28th the entire division was relieved and moved back behind the line. The Battle of Loos had cost the 8th Black Watch 19 officers, of whom nine were killed, and 492 other ranks were killed and wounded.

In June 1916, after many months of trench warfare in the Ypres Salient, the heavily reinforced 8th moved onto the Somme where a final draft of ten newly commissioned second lieutenants joined the battalion on 20th June. Five of them, Hastings, Hutton, McRae, Mc A. Cameron and Tindal, now had less than a month to live. At 7 p.m. on 13th July the 8th moved forward to Breslau Alley trench in preparation for the attack on the following morning.

Below: Black Watch at Delville Wood.

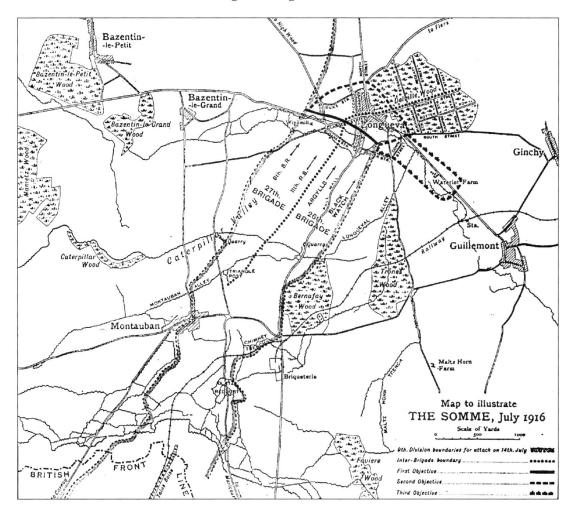

117

The 9th Division's objective was the capture of Longueval and Delville Wood and the Highland Brigade was detailed to take the southern portion of the village and to include Waterlot Farm and then push on through the wood. The advance in the 26th Brigade sector would be led by the Black Watch on the right, with the 10th Argyle and Sutherland Highlanders on the left; 7th Seaforth supporting and 5th Camerons in reserve. At 11 p.m. on the 13th the battalion filed out from Breslau trench and by 3 a.m. the next morning had moved into position on the slopes of Longueval, some 400 yards south of the village. The ground on which the battalion lay was heavily shelled during the night and the Scots were obliged to move further forward in order to avoid more casualties.

At 3.25 a.m. on the 14th the first wave of attackers rushed forward to assault Longueval and after severe fighting all objectives were taken, with the exception of a strong point on the south east of the village which was not captured until 5 p.m. After the fall of Longueval, patrols were sent into Devil's Wood and met little resistance but by afternoon strong German reinforcements had arrived and the Scots were driven back.

Below: Delville Wood, British official photograph taken in September 1916.

Furthermore, enemy artillery saturated the village with shell fire throughout the day and the battalion was forced to evacuate several advanced, exposed, posts. In addition, casualties were mounting. All four company commanders were dead or wounded and there were substantial losses among the rank and file. By nightfall German troops had filtered back into the northern outskirts of the village.

For the next three days the situation was unchanged but the village was still subjected to constant shelling and the 8th had lost so many men that on the 17th the battle reserve was sent up from the transport lines to reinforce the survivors. That night approaching Longueval, the battalion's wheeled transport and ration parties were caught in a storm of high explosive and gas shells; there were grievous losses among both personnel and animals.

On the 18th at 4 a.m. the 2nd Gordons, assisted by 'A' and 'D' companies of the Black Watch, attacked without artillery preparation and recaptured the northern part of the village. This success was followed by a violent enemy bombardment on Longueval and Delville Wood which continued for ten hours. Under cover of this barrage the Germans launched a strong thrust at 3 p.m. and regained Devil's Wood and most of the village. 'A' and 'D' companies were driven from the northern outskirts of the village and back to the railway line, but here the whole battalion rallied and checked the enemy advance. A Scottish counter-attack not only cleared the village but also succeeded in gaining a foothold in the wood, but here the attackers were outflanked. As a consequence the battalion, having suffered heavy losses, was forced to retire to Clarges Street. That evening a South African trench mortar company moved up in support and enabled the surviving Scots to hold their ground.

Early on the 19th the 8th was relieved and moved back behind the lines - the battalion mustered six officers and 165 rank and file some of them wounded. Nine officers had been killed, 14 wounded, two had died of wounds and three were missing. Of the other ranks, eight were killed, 370 wounded, 13 had died of wounds and 71 were missing (many of the missing subsequently reported as dead).

Reinforced time and time again the 8th had yet to live through, or die in, the Battles of Arras, Passchendaele and the German Spring Offensive of March 1918.

18
The Lucky Seventh
1/7th Middlesex, Battle of Flers-Courcelette, 15th September 1916

In August 1914 all the officers and men of the 1/7th Battalion, Middlesex Regiment volunteered for overseas service, as befitted one of the senior Territorial battalions of the British Army. They were rather disgusted therefore to find themselves landing in Gibraltar on 10th September 1914, ready to defend Britain's key to the Mediterranean. However, by 1915 trained troops were in short supply and in February the 1/7th embarked for the Western Front, via England. On their way to the docks the 1/7th passed its sister battalion, the 2/7th, which had just landed in Gibraltar, This was the only occasion during the war when the two units were to meet.

After training in England the 1/7th, with a strength of 31 officers and 904 other ranks, landed in France where it was posted to the 23rd Infantry Brigade of the 8th Division. On 9th May 1915 the battalion participated in the Battle of Aubers Ridge, albeit in supporting role, and escaped with the extraordinarily light casualty returns of 15 killed and 37 wounded. The 1/7th was promptly dubbed 'The Lucky Seventh' and retained the nickname until late in 1916. At the beginning of February 1916 the 1/7th was transferred to the 167th Infantry Brigade of the newly formed 56th Division. For much of 1916 the battalion was engaged in the usual round of trench warfare, broken by rest periods out of the line. Unfortunately the restful times were usually devoted to humping supplies or something really asinine such as polishing up the men's saluting drill. On the first day of the Somme the unit played a diversionary role in the Gommecourt Salient which cost it 150 killed and wounded.

The third phase of the frightful Somme battles of 1916 was now about to begin. Nine divisions of the Fourth Army were to attack west of Combles with the object of capturing Morval, Les Boeufs Guedecourt and Flers. The 56th Division was on the extreme right of the line with orders to clear Bouleaux Wood and form a protective flank blocking Combles; an operation which was straightforward on paper but not in practice. In Bouleaux Wood only a small portion of the southern end was not in enemy hands and the front line ran in a north-westerly direction to the Ginchy-Morval road, where it bent back due west and then followed the line of the road to the eastern exits from Ginchy. Thus, parts of the right flank faced east, north-east and due north!

Objectives allotted to the 167th Brigade were, (a) the front line German trench astride Bouleaux Wood, and (b) the enemy line from the northern corner of the wood to the junction with 169th Brigade just north of the Combles-Ginchy road. The 1st (City of London Battalion would deal with (a) and the 1/7th would attack (b).

In the forthcoming Battle of Flers-Courcelette there would be two firsts; the use of tanks, three were allotted to the 56th Division, and the introduction of a creeping barrage. This latter was an artillery fire plan which protected assaulting infantry by shelling each successive enemy line immediately ahead of the advancing troops and timed to the attackers' rate of progress on foot. The barrage moved forward by 'lifts,' usually 50 yards at a time, with the shelling between 'lifts' usually lasting $1\frac{1}{2}$ minutes. Viewed from the rear, at a distance, the barrage appeared to creep forward, hence the name. This worked well except where the P.B.I. were held up and the barrage, being fired to a strict timetable, drew away from them, or where troops in their eagerness and the confusion of battle came to close to their own barrage and suffered losses from 'shorts.'

On the night of 14th September 1916 troops of the 167th Brigade moved into their battle positions with the 1/7th in the assembly trenches in the western edge of Leuze Wood. 'A' Company (Captain Woodroffe) on the right and Capt. Tulley's 'C' Company on the left would spearhead the Middlesex with 'B' and 'D' in support. The 1st Londoners would be the first to move.

At 6.20 a.m. on the 15th as the British bombardment peaked the Londoners jumped off. They succeeded in taking a portion of the German front line that lay astride and to the left of Bouleaux Wood, but suffered heavy losses in the attempt and were finally brought to a standstill. At 8.20 a.m. the 1/7th were ordered to push the two leading companies forward to leapfrog the 1st London and clear the wood. Reaching the line held by their fellow Londoners they carried the survivors with them for a short distance until they also were pinned down. Not only was the wood filled with enemy riflemen but murderous enfilade machine-gun fire from the direction of the Combles road tore gaps in the ranks of the attackers. On the right, 'A' Company was practically destroyed and only 25 men survived. Capt. Woodroffe fell dead, shot through the head, and his three subalterns had all fallen, one dead, one mortally and one severely wounded. The left hand company 'C' slightly sheltered from the enfilade fire, had suffered less severely but had still lost all their officers. Capt. Tulley lay dying and his subalterns were among the casualties, one dead and the other two badly wounded.

The two support companies, 'B' and 'D,' were then thrown in with orders that the attack was to be driven home 'at all costs.' 'B' on the left was led by Capt. Hanbury and Capt. Hurd's 'D' Company was on the right. Capt. Hurd positioned his Lewis gunners to damp down the enfilade fire but as he was directing them he was shot through the head and died two days later. 'B' Company was temporarily checked by withering enemy fire until Capt. Hanbury led them forward only to fall

Below: 1/7th Middlesex, Battle of Flers Courcelette, 15th-22nd September 1916.

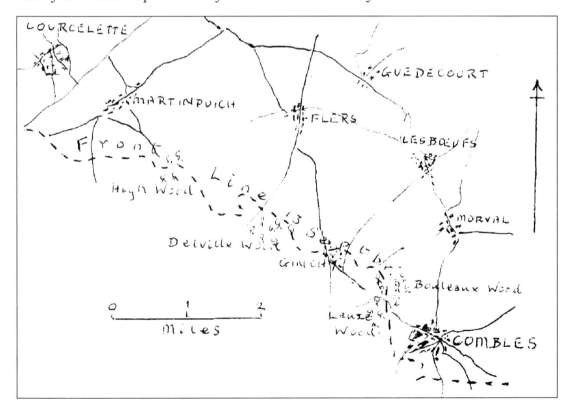

dead on the edge of the German trench. The 'Lucky Seventh' had now lost 13 officers, including the four company commanders, and the entire attack had been brought to a standstill. Desultory sniping and bombing continued for the rest of the day with both sides licking their wounds. That night the 1/7th took over the old front-line trenches running through the southern edge of Bouleaux Wood. A few hours earlier the battalion had gone into action some 500 strong and had since lost 300, including 13 officers of whom ten had been killed, as had 13 of the other ranks.

On the 19th the 167th Brigade was relieved but returned to the reserve trenches on the 22nd, the day the battle officially closed. Whilst out of the line the 1/7th (no longer regarded as 'The Lucky Seventh') received a large draft of reinforcements; just in time for the Battle of Le Transloy Ridges. These ridges lay about 3,000 yards north-east of Les Boeufs and when the battle opened on 1st October 1916 the 167th and 169th Brigades were ordered to establish a line of posts over the crest of the ridge along the Divisional front.

Under cover of a shrapnel barrage the 1/7th pushed forward an officer and 20 men from each of the four companies to place four posts some 700 yards in front. That evening an extra post was added in order to cover the exposed left flank of the battalion and all the posts were then linked up by a trench and wired. Two officers were wounded and 20 rank and file killed or wounded during this exercise. In order that the 1/7th might be rested before zero day, which was fixed for the 5th, the battalion, including the garrisons of the posts, was relieved by another unit on the night of the 3rd. One of the posts, held by Lieut. Prockter and 17 men, was duly relieved and the party marched off only to lose its way in the pitch black darkness and stumble into the German trenches. Although surrounded the group refused to surrender and fought it out hand to hand until the subaltern and 12 of his men had been killed and the remaining five, all wounded, were taken prisoner. This was the first occasion that any 1/7th personnel had been captured by the enemy.

Atrocious weather with heavy rain turned the trenches and No-Man's-Land into a sticky morass and forced a postponement of the attack until 7th October. The battalion's objective was Spectrum Trench and the formation of a line of posts beyond. Just before zero hour at 1.45 p.m. a creeping barrage of shrapnel descended on the enemy trenches which were some 400 yards from the 1/7th's position. Under cover of the barrage the Middlesex men went over the top - 'D' Company on the right under Lieut. Groser, 'C' on the left led by 2/Lieut. Moss and the supporting companies, 'B' under Lieut. King and 'A' commanded by 2/Lieut. Williams.

The two leading companies reached the German front line and carried it almost at once. Some of the men were in the trenches bombing and bayoneting the enemy while others remained on the parapet shooting down on any German who presented himself. The arrival of the support companies minutes later completed the clearance and 77 unwounded Germans and many wounded were sent back as prisoners. However, the 1/7th paid heavily for their success; both company commanders of 'C' and 'D' were dead, as were two other subalterns and two more had been wounded. Of the other ranks 183 had been killed or wounded out of an attacking force of 450.

No further attacks were made by the 1/7th in their weakened state, but on the 8th the 3rd Londoners made an unsuccessful attempt take the remainder of Spectrum Trench. During the bombardment which preceded this attack the 1/7th lost some 30 men from the friendly fire of their own artillery. On the next day the battalion moved out of the line and lost another officer. 2/Lieut. Webster, age 19, and obviously born under an unlucky star, had survived the attack on Spectrum Trench only to be killed by one stray bullet fired from a German aeroplane.

The 1/7th, constantly reinforced, continued to serve on the Western Front until the end of the war, but by November 1918 only a handful of men were left who remembered Gibraltar.

19
The Suicide Squad
151 Machine-Gun Company on the Ancre, 5th November 1916

When war was declared every British infantry battalion had its own machine-gun section of two Maxims served by twelve other ranks, who were usually marksmen with a rifle, commanded by a subaltern. It soon became obvious that two guns were woefully inadequate to back a unit of some 900 men, often deployed on a wide frontage, and the Machine-gun Corps was formed by Royal Warrant on 14th October 1915. Shortly afterwards the Maxim was replaced by the Vickers machine-gun. Although the machine-gunners were not infantry as such they were certainly front line troops who accompanied the first wave of every attack and remained behind to cover every retirement.

However, despite being picked men, there were certain disadvantages in belonging to the new Corps. Before October 1915 machine-gunners wishing to report sick paraded before the medical officer of the battalion in which they served, but when the Corps was inaugurated there was no establishment for a doctor with a machine-gun company. Hence the sufferer reported to the M.O. of the nearest unit who confronted with a strange soldier and being wary of lead-swingers, would often prescribe medicine and duty. Medicine in this case usually consisted of the British Army's panacea for all ills - the No.9 pill. Number 9's were expected to cure trench feet, toothache, ingrowing toenails, scabies and rat bites, in addition to regulating the pulse and healing boils in private places on the body.

Among the major disadvantages was the fact that a machine-gun company invariably attracted the attention of any enemy artillery or trench mortar crew within range. Probably this was the reason that the Corps was known to the B.P.I. as 'The Suicide Squad.' By the end of the war a total of 170,500 officers and men had served in the Machine-gun Corps and, of these, 62,049 had become casualties.

One of the lesser known battles of the war in which the machine-gunners were heavily involved was the attack by the

Durham Brigade (officially the 151st Infantry Brigade) on the Butte-de-Warlencourt on 5th November 1916. The Somme battles were dragging to a close but preparations were in hand for the Fifth Army to attack north of Ancre on 12th November over ground that had not been churned by heavy shelling; but before this assault could be launched there was a serious obstacle to overcome. This was the Butte-de-Warlencourt, a chalk mound sixty feet high, which dominated the surrounding flat ground and allowed the Germans to observe the entire Ancre sector.

Above: Butte de Warlencourt; photograph taken in the 1930s.

This strange crater-pocked freak was graphically described by C.E. Carrington in *A Subaltern's War* who wrote, 'To go or come from the line was a nightmare adventure and, once there, one dared not move for fear of the enemy machine-guns on the Butte of Warlencourt. That ghastly hill, never free from the smoke of bursting shells, became fabulous. It shone white in the night and seemed to leer at you like an ogre in a fairy tale. It loomed up unexpectedly, peering into trenches where you thought yourself safe; it haunted your dreams. Twenty-four hours in the trenches before the Butte finished a man off.'

However, before any attacking troops even reached the barbed wire, the trenches and the machine-gun nests that defended the Butte, they had first to fight their way across a sea of mud. According to Brian Gardner, author of *The Big Push*, 'As they carried out orders to attack the Butte, troops slipped and slithered in the mud and fell into water-logged shell holes. Some who were too exhausted to go further, sank down and were left to perish. Others lost their boots, and even socks, in the ooze. One unit arrived at the German trenches without a boot or sock between them. One officer lost his trousers as well. These last facts are all recorded in the *Official History*; there are many witnesses to drowning in mud.'

Nevertheless, as far as the top brass was concerned, it was imperative that the hill fortress be captured before the main attack went in on the 12th November.

Three infantry battalions were assigned to the task - the 9th Durham Light Infantry opposite the Butte, the 6th D.L.I. in the centre and the 8th Durhams on the right flank. The 151st Machine-gun Company and 151st Trench Mortar Battery would give the infantry close support. Two Vickers guns were to go forward with each battalion, leaving six guns behind for overhead fire and four in reserve - 16 guns in all. Zero hour for the ground troops was 9.10 a.m. after a ten minute artillery bombardment to soften up the enemy defenders and destroy some of the barbed wire surrounding the Butte. Presumably someone remembered that it was the anniversary of the Gunpowder Plot and made the appropriate remarks about fireworks.

Punctually at 9.10 a.m. in vile wet and windy weather the infantry and machine-gunners went over the top. On the right flank an Australian brigade was to assist on the right of the 8th Durhams but the Aussies, along with the 8th and machine-gun crews, immediately bogged down in No-Man's Land floundering knee deep through thick glutinous mud. Many were unable to move at all and were shot down as they struggled. In the centre the 6th Durhams fared little better and the machine-gunners, struggling through the mud and laden down with their guns, tripods and ammunition boxes were left behind and sustained many casualties. Perversely, only in the most exposed position of all, in the centre, did the attack succeed and the 9th, despite heavy losses, took the Butte. It appears that the men of the 6th and 8th, in their struggles to push forward, had attracted much of the enemy fire.

When the hill was captured, Cpl. Rutherford, 'B' Section, advancing with the 9th Durhams set up his gun on the Bapaume road but shortly afterwards he and his men were knocked out and Cpl. Mewes' gun team, also with the 9th, suffered a similar fate. Both flanks were in the air and Sgt. Glennall, Cpl. Watson and Cpl. Butler went forward with their guns and teams from the support line in order to cover the exposed flanks. These three teams played a vital role in repulsing the first German counter-attack at about 11 p.m. that night. Sgt. Leith had also moved into position with his team but they were all killed or wounded in the first minutes of the night action. Although badly wounded himself, Leith crawled back to the old front line and refused medical attention until his wounded team mates were rescued. An entire German Guards Division had been rushed up from Bapaume to take part in the second counter-attack at midnight on the 5th and these elite enemy troops were supported by artillery of army corps strength. This second attack was beaten off but the casualty roll among the Durhams was now assuming horrendous proportions and most of the defensive fire came from the machine-guns.

Early next morning, the 6th, the corporal of the second gun team was killed as he left his trench and for the rest of that day Pte. Hay kept the gun in action with only one other gunner, wounded, to assist him (the other members of the team were already dead). Cpl. Monty Watson of 'A' Section with a gun team supporting what was left of the 9th Durhams in a captured German trench had fired off so many belts of ammunition that he was short of rounds but at this point a Durham captain climbed to the top of the Butte and discovered the reinforced Germans massing for another attack. There were so few Durhams left that they would never beat off another mass assault, even with the aid of the machine-gunners, and the officer ordered his men and the gunners to return to their original trenches. Cpl. Watson was instructed to move his gun back to the old position immediately.

Watson uncoupled the gun and turned round to find his surviving team member, Pte. McRoberts, holding a revolver (machine-gunners carried revolvers instead of rifles) to the ribs of a Prussian Guardsman who had somehow found his way to the rear of the machine-gun post. The gun and the guardsman were safely removed back down the hill to 151 M.G.H.Q. where the prisoner gave some valuable information. The Germans swarmed back onto the Butte and late that night the survivors of the Durham Brigade were relieved by 150th Brigade.

Corporal Watson was a coal miner from Durham who joined the 6th Durham Territorial Battalion before the outbreak of war and became a member of the machine-gun section late in 1914. Around Christmas 1915 he transferred to the newly formed Machine-gun Corps and was posted to the 151 Machine-gun Company with whom he served until 17th May 1918 when he was seriously wounded during the Battle of the Aisne. By that time he was a sergeant and the holder of a Military Medal and bar. With both legs smashed and his section guns destroyed by shell fire he ordered the few remaining gunners to withdraw and leave him. The Germans took him prisoner and patched him up.

Sgt. Watson survived the war and in 1939 when the second conflict broke out he became an officer in command of a Home Guard machine-gun section - despite his disability.

In 1917, when the Germans retired to the Hindenburg Line, the Butte-de-Warlencourt was finally occupied by the British and the Durham Brigade erected a cross on the Butte in memory of the men who died there on 5 November 1916. The cross now lies in Durham Cathedral.

20
Frankfurt Trench
16th Highland Light Infantry, Battle of the Ancre, 18th November 1916

The 16th Highland Light Infantry had been well and truly blooded on that catastrophic first day of the Somme battles which cost the Glasgow Boys Brigade Battalion over two-thirds of its strength, including 20 out of 25 officers. Now, on 18th November 1916, heavily reinforced, mostly from the Highland Cyclist Battalion, the Glaswegians peered through swirling snow at the heights of Beaumont-Hamel. At 6.10 a.m. the British barrage lifted and each man, laden down with half a hundredweight of arms and equipment, including six bombs, 220 rounds of ammunition and a trenching spade, heaved himself out of the jump-off trench and into No-Man's-Land.

On the left flank, the 2nd Manchesters, 2nd KOYLI and the 11th Border Regiment, after initial successes, were heavily counter-attacked and beaten back. On the battalion's half right front an enemy strong point with six to eight machine-guns pinned down 'A' and 'B' Companies. Only 'C' and 'D' Companies on the half left penetrated Munich trench, the German front line. Three platoons of 'D' Company, leaving the remainder to clear their captured trench, pushed on to their second objective, Frankfurt trench. Despite heavy shelling and vicious machine-gun fire this second trench was stormed and its 50 surviving defenders made prisoners and sent back under escort. This

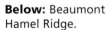

Below: Beaumont Hamel Ridge.

group reached Munich trench in time for the guards to be shot down and the prisoners freed as the mopping-up party, attacked from three sides by overwhelming numbers, was rushed and destroyed.

The attempted capture of the German first and second line trenches and the subsequent command of the Beaumont-Hamel spur had failed after heavy casualties (the 16th alone had lost 13 officers and 390 rank and file). Now, with Munich trench cleared, the Germans no doubt thought that the 32nd Division's attack had been completely repulsed. However, unbeknown to the enemy, a battered remnant of Frankfurt trench was still held by three officers and about 60 other ranks of the 16th H.L.I., together with a few men of the 11th Borders. This group, with Munich trench once more firmly held by the enemy, was now deeply implanted in German territory.

By nightfall a number of stragglers had reached Frankfurt trench and the community had grown to about 45 effectives and a similar number of wounded. A dusk reconnaissance revealed that the trenches in front and to the rear, together with the

Below: 16th Highland Light Infantry at the Ancre.

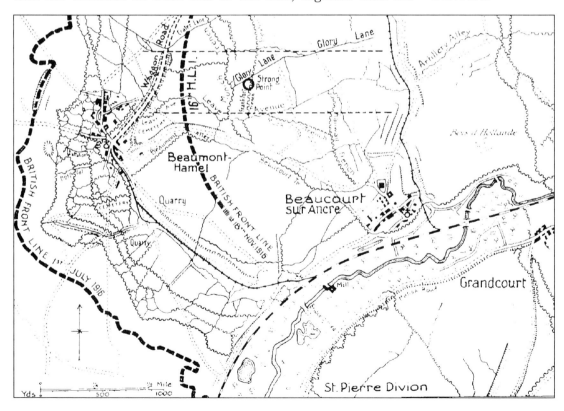

communication alleys on either flank, were occupied by Germans and the garrison was isolated with very limited resources. Two dugouts still existed in the battered trench, one was allocated to the corporal in charge of the wounded and the fit men were accommodated in the second. There were four Lewis guns but only a limited number of rounds, which were implemented from bandoliers of the dead lying in the open. In addition, the men handed their own small arms ammunition to the machine-gunners and then armed themselves with captured German Mauser rifles and cartridges. The machine-gun N.C.O., Lance Corporal Veitch, the son of a sergeant in the Scots Greys and a survivor of the Somme holocaust, was to prove himself a tower of strength and be recommended for the V.C. Bombs were not too plentiful and both food and water were scarce, but in worst case of all were the wounded. There were not enough field dressings available to cover all the mangled flesh and, apart from occasionally easing the sufferer's position, nothing could be done for those unfortunates with broken bones and limbs.

By the second day the garrison had settled to a state of siege. Collapsing trench walls had been revetted and machine-gun emplacements established at vital points. The senior N.C.O., Sergeant Lee, a Glasgow Corporation roads foreman before the war and an original member of the battalion, cheered and encouraged his men throughout the day. He too would later be recommended for the Victoria Cross. That night a sergeant of the 11th Borders managed to creep through the enemy lines in an attempt to bring succour to the besieged.

At dawn on the third day, supported by trench mortar fire and bombs, the Germans made a determined attempt to wipe out the puny garrison. By the time the surviving attackers melted away the balance of strength in the trench had shifted and there were now more wounded than fit men. Accordingly the line was shortened, the smaller dugout evacuated and, after dark, the routine search for shell-hole water assumed a fresh urgency. That night a heavy British barrage fell around the garrison but after the first bursts of small arms fire there was silence; the first relief attempt had failed.

Fresh hope came on the fourth day when torch signals flashed from British planes urged the men in Frankfurt trench to hold out as help was on the way. The fifth day saw the promised relief force beaten back with over 300 casualties. Once again the garrison was driven underground by heavy shelling which blew in the dugout entrances and destroyed much of the revetting. Conditions in the trench were rapidly worsening. Many of the wounds were gangrenous, and lack of food and sleep was blunting the efficiency of those men still unwounded. On the afternoon of the sixth day, November 23rd, the Germans launched a powerful attack from front and flanks which nearly succeeded. Unusually heavy shelling and the sentries' warnings aroused the defenders, but it was difficult for exhausted men to run up half-destroyed dugout steps. After a hand-to-hand struggle using entrenching tools and bayonets the Germans were routed, leaving behind them eight prisoners. One of the heaviest blows to the defence was the loss of the indefatigable L/Cpl. Veitch, after the fight was over, killed by a sniper's bullet as he manned his Lewis gun.

On the morning of the seventh day an Inniskilling Fusilier, captured in one of the unsuccessful relief attempts, appeared waving a white flag with a message from the German divisional commander. Roughly translated it read, 'Surrender and get good treatment or stay where you are and be killed.' After a short pause, presumably for reflection, the occupants of Frankfurt trench were subjected to the heaviest shelling they had yet endured; one of the casualties was Sergeant Lee, killed by shrapnel. That night the searchers found a pool of precious water and several bottles were stealthily filled and passed back into the trench. However, when it was poured it was so discoloured and gave off such a villainous stench that the corporal in charge of the wounded refused to give it to his patients, in spite of their pleas. It was just as well - those who drank it contracted a virulent form of typhoid.

The promised German attack came on the eighth day, in force and from every point of the compass. Sentries and machine-gunners were shot down or bombed as the listless effectives struggled out from the dugout. The process of sheer annihilation was only halted by screams from the eight enemy prisoners. The last stand of 'D' Company of the 16th Highland Light Infantry was over. Fifteen sick and exhausted men stumbled into captivity; the remainder were painfully manhandled out on stretchers or buried where they lay. Two of the wounded died on their way to prison camp and yet another was shot by the Germans for accepting a piece of bread from a Frenchwoman.

In 1919 the recommendation under Army Order 193 was sponsored by no less a personage than General Sir Hubert Gough, G.O.C. of the Fifth Army. The closing sentence of his letter to the War Office reads, 'I consider that these men deserve great recognition for the magnificent example of soldierly qualities they displayed.'

It seems probable that every survivor was decorated because the 16th received one D.S.O., two M.C.s, eleven D.C.M.s and twenty-two M.M.s - the highest number of awards by far, for a single action to any one battalion. The two N.C.O.s, both recommended for the V.C., each received a posthumous mention in despatches!

D.S.O.
Lieut. John Stewart.

M.C.
2/Lieutenant Malcolm Murray
    Lyon
2/Lieutenant Frank Scott

D.C.M.
14952 Cpl. Browne
14811 Sgt. Buchan
3579 L/Cpl. Eastop
14661 L/Cpl. Fletcher
43183 Pte. Fraser
26203 L/Cpl. McArthur
14493 Pte. McLay
27274 Pte. Manson
43155 Pte. Millar
14388 Pte. Mitchell
43163 Pte. Smart

M.M.
27252 Pte. Cairns
3563 Pte. Duncanson

28779 Pte Grant
9345 Pte. Gunning
40546 Pte. Hay
43144 Pte. Hughes
45105 Cpl. Lamb
32681 L/Cpl. McAllister
24571 Pte. McBride
27250 Pte. McGregor
14823 Pte. McGrottie
30325 Pte. McKinley
1451 Pte. McInnes
3524 Pte. McPhee
27270 Pte. Manson
14398 Cpl. Reid
43181 Pte. Shaw
43262 Pte.Smart
14287 Pte. Smith
30306 Pte. Stevenson
40542 Pte. Steward
43165 Pte. Whittet

Mentioned in Despatches
15154 Sgt Lee
14545 L/Cpl. Veitch

21
A Most Remarkable Man
1st King's Own Scottish Borderers, Second Battle Langemarck, 16th August 1917

Zero hour at 4.45 a.m. on 16th August 1917 marked the beginning of the second Battle of Langemarck, and the 1st Battalion, King's Own Scottish Borderers, part of the 87th Infantry Brigade of the 29th Division, was attacking on a frontage of 800 yards. 'A' Company was on the left with the acting C.S.M., John Skinner, well out in front as usual. He had joined the regiment in 1900 as a lad 16 years old and had fought in the Boer War in which he had been wounded three times. A man of proven courage, he had won the D.C.M. in the Ypres salient back in October 1914.

The first enemy line had been taken and consolidated, but as the Borderers approached the second objective, in front of the Steenbeek, their attack bogged down under heavy machine-gun fire from the left. Then, in the words of the *London Gazette*, Skinner 'collected six men and with great courage and determi-

Left: German block-house in the Ypres Salient, 1917.

134

Above: C.S.M. John Skinner V.C., D.C.M.

nation worked round the left flank of three block-houses from which machine-gun fire was coming, and succeeded in bombing and taking the first blockhouse single-handed; then leading his six men towards the other two blockhouses he skilfully cleared them, taking 60 prisoners, three machine-guns and two trench mortars. The dash and gallantry displayed by this warrant officer enabled the objective to be reached and consolidated.'

What the *Gazette* failed to mention was the fact that Skinner had been wounded (for the sixth time since 1914) just before his latest exploit. Nor the fact that he had crawled 70 yards by himself - the journey took ten minutes under heavy shell and machine-gun fire all the time - before he could come to grips with the defenders of the first blockhouse. He took the second pillbox by pushing Mills bombs through the loopholes from which the German guns were being fired.

Skinner was awarded the Victoria Cross and returned to England for the investiture and the usual 14 days leave granted on such occasions. He was then posted as an instructor to the reserve battalion at Edinburgh where he could have stayed for the rest of the war. However, Skinner was not only a fighting soldier but he and his friend Quartermaster Sergeant Victor Ross (eight times wounded), who was back in the battalion, had a wager as to who would be the first to receive another wound. Skinner disobeyed orders and returned to the Front where he won his bet but lost his life. On 17th March 1918 he was sniped and killed while rescuing a wounded soldier.

Two days later an immaculate gun carriage drawn by four carefully groomed horses carried the coffin of Company Sergeant Major Skinner, V.C., D.C.M. , Croix de Guerre avec Palme, to the New British Cemetery at Vlamertinghe. He was borne to his grave by six Victoria Cross holders acting as pall bearers, and six generals marched in the cortege through teeming rain. It was an impressive funeral worthy of a soldier described in the regimental history as 'one of the most remarkable men in the British Army.'

22
Council of War
13th Essex, Battle of Cambrai, 26th November 1917

On 23rd January 1915 *The Stratford Express* carried the following notice, '13th (Service) Battalion Essex Regiment (West Ham): No Gas Bag Invasion can alarm us. True manhood will win. Join your friends in the West Ham Battalion who have already enlisted (names follow). Men resident in the Borough are being billeted at home. Allowance 2s. per day; immediate equipment. - HENRY DYER, Mayor.' The newly raised unit was promptly nicknamed 'The Hammers' after the West Ham Football Club. Early in March over 1,000 men had enlisted and by the end of that month the 13th was over-strength with 1,300 all ranks.

After initial training the battalion embarked on the *Princess Victoria* at Folkestone Harbour on 17th November 1915. As they left the harbour, recruits lining the top deck saw war at second-hand when the auxiliary hospital ship *Anglia* was mined a mile east of Folkestone Gate and sank within ten minutes taking with her a nurse and 133 wounded soldiers. The sinking occurred about 12.30 p.m. and was witnessed by the crew of a collier which steamed to the assistance of *Anglia* and lowered two boats. These had just pulled away from the side of the vessel when the collier herself struck another mine and began to sink. The trooper was eventually allowed to proceed, after minesweepers had swept the area, and the 13th Essex reached Boulogne at 6 o'clock that evening.

After trench instruction the battalion was moved to Bethune on 22nd December 1915 and transferred into the 6th Infantry Brigade, 2nd Division, with which it would remain until 1918. The 2nd was one of the most famous Divisions of the 'Old Contemptibles'; it had held the line at Mons, and subsequent actions at Ypres, Neuve Chapelle, Festubert and Loos saw it in the thick of the fighting.

Throughout 1916 and much of 1917 the record of the 13th was steady rather than spectacular, although it came in for its fair share of action which was reflected in the casualty lists. The battalion fought at Givenchy in January, Festubert the following month, and thence to Lens. Fortunately the 13th missed the opening stages of the 1916 Somme offensive which crippled so many of Kitchener's new battalions but it fought at Delville Wood on 27th July and took part in the attack on Beaumont-Hamel in November. This last action cost the men of West Ham ten officers killed and two wounded, 149 other ranks killed or wounded, and another 165 missing. Of the latter only seven were subsequently reported a prisoners of war, the other 142 were among the dead. In the Battle of Arleux on 28/29th April 1917 the battalion suffered seven officers killed and four wounded. Figures for the rank and file showed 82 killed or wounded and 240 reported as missing, most of whom were later returned as killed. When the Division was relieved on 4th May the parade state for the 13th named only 12 officers and 423 men. Shortly afterwards the battalion was reinforced (for the fourth time) with a draft of four officers and 159 rank and file.

For the remainder of the year the battalion rotated between tours of duty in the trenches and, especially for the many recruits, training out of the line. On 31st October 1917 the effective strength stood at 39 officers and 1,072 other ranks, with a fighting strength of 39 officers and 884 men. On 22nd November the 13th received a warning order to be ready to move to an unknown destination. The transfer was completed by the 26th and that night the 2nd Division took over from the 36th Division, south west of Bourlon village, with the 6th Infantry Brigade on the left. The Battle of Cambrai had started on 20th November and although strong enemy reinforcements had stopped any further British advance there was still heavy fighting in progress for the possession of Bourlon Wood and the village, which had been alternately won and lost. On the night of the 26th most of the wood and the high ground to the north-west of it remained in British hands but Bourlon village was still held by the Germans.

The line held by 6th Brigade was cut through the centre by the Canal du Nord which ran from south to north, not only through the brigade sector but also through the German positions east of Moeuvres. This enabled the enemy to enfilade the bridges across the canal from their trenches. The Canal du Nord was about 30 feet deep, 80 feet broad at the top and narrowed to 40 feet at the bottom. However, it was still under construction; hence the bed of the canal was dry and runners were able to cross the obstacle by sliding down the 30 foot wall and then hauling themselves up the other side by means of a rope. Although the feat was performed under enemy machine-gun and rifle fire it was rather less dangerous than attempting to run the gauntlet across one of the bridges. The 13th was on the Brigade's right, with 'D' Company under Capt. Jessop occupying trenches on the western side of the canal while Capt. Keeble's 'B' Company garrisoned Lock No.5 and dug and occupied small trenches on the northern and eastern edges of the Lock. 'A' Company supported 'B' and 'C' was in the same relationship to 'D' Company.

At dawn on 30th November the Germans put down a barrage on the 13th's sector which increased in severity until 9.30 a.m. when enemy infantry made a determined onslaught from several positions, chiefly the Moeuvres-Bourlon road and along the sunken road from Moeuvres. 'B' Company took the brunt of the main thrust directed at Lock No.5 and beat it back, but expended nearly all its small arms ammunition and Mills bombs. Fortunately a cache of 300 rounds was discovered in a dugout by the sunken road and most of this was loaded into the Lewis gun magazines. Meanwhile three sections of the reserve platoon, plus a Vickers heavy machine-gun, lined the sunken road, facing north-east, and a fourth section held the bridge

Below: 'Council of War' – 13th Essex at Cambrai.
Thick broken line indicates the approximate British front line on 30th November 1917.

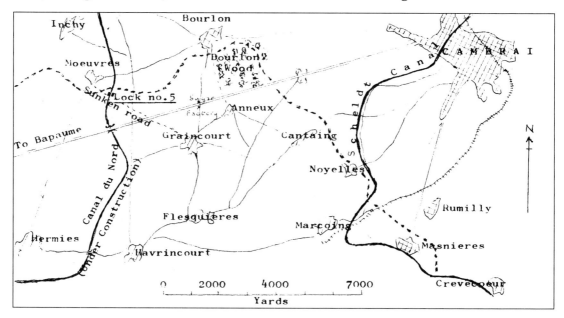

with its front towards the north and north-west. It was difficult to estimate the enemy's strength but at one time about 600 to 700 men had been seen attacking in formation.

'D' Company was still in its first position in trenches west of the canal at 10.20 a.m. but five minutes later the situation suddenly worsened and British troops on the far right of 'D' could be seen retiring under heavy shelling. At 10.30 a.m. there was another attack by German infantry from the north-east and once again 'B' Company was nearly out of ammunition until 2/Lieut. Hall arrived with a platoon from 'A' Company carrying several boxes of S.A.A. This extra support was used to extend the line to the right, but as most of the men were in the open they soon became casualties.

Finally the position became so critical that the remainder of 'B' Company, now reduced to 40 men, who had expended all their grenades and ammunition for the third time, were forced to retreat. They managed to retire through the sunken road at the bridge taking with them the unwounded men of the reinforcing platoon from 'A' and the six survivors of the bridge garrison. Among the killed was Lieut. Hall. This group was closely followed by the enemy who immediately occupied Lock 5 and that part of the sunken road.

The remainder of the West Ham men, with assistance from the 2nd South Staffordshires, counter-attacked and the tide of battle ebbed to and fro all day. 'C' Company in particular was heavily engaged and by 4 p.m. it had been reduced to two officers and 15 rank and file. Meanwhile, nothing had been heard of 'D' Company and written orders were sent to Captain Jessop, O.C. 'D,' that if he had been driven out of his position he was to establish a new defence line running west from the bridge. This instruction was rather different to his previous verbal order to hold his position at all costs. In any case the written order never reached him - he was cut off from the rest of the battalion.

At 8 p.m. Sgt. Legg and another man, having made their way through the encircling Germans, reported to Battalion H.Q. with news of their beleaguered comrades. The saga of 'D' Company had started at 8.45 that morning when the position was heavily shelled and 2/Lieut. Corps, officer of the watch, reported that the enemy were lined up in waves, about 1,000 yards away, ready to attack. S.O.S. flares, to which British artillery responded, were fired and the men went to their battle stations leaving just one sentry in each fire bay. Fortunately, the

German gunners were overestimating the range and there were few casualties but Captain Steele, the 2nd i/c was one of the unfortunate few.

Masses of German infantry shook out into artillery formation and attacked. Dead and broken ground favoured their advance and twice they reached within 200 yards of 'D' Company's trenches and twice they were beaten back by vigorous Lewis gun and rifle fire. They then ceased to assault en masse and began to infiltrate bombing parties into the canal and sunken roads. About 11 a.m. the situation worsened and the enemy could be seen on both flanks of the Company's position, the other British troops having been forced to retire. Telephone wires to Battalion H.Q. had been cut early in the action and runners sent out with news of the Company plight had been killed or captured. About this time Captain Jessop was wounded and command of the company devolved on Lieut. Robinson with 2/Lieut. Corps as the only other effective officer.

By noon the enemy had strengthened his hold on the canal and Germans were also in the rear of 'D' Company's trenches. Although the company snipers continued to harass their opponents, ammunition supplies were running low and two counter-attacks were made with the bayonet. In one of these sorties 13 German bombers, attempting to work their way along the canal bed, were captured. At 4.30 p.m. there was a great deal of aerial activity involving both British and German planes and the company tried to signal its plight by morse S.O.S. messages.

Now, in a scene reminiscent of the Middle Ages, the two officers, Edwards the company sergeant major, and platoon sergeants Phil Parsons, Fairbrass, Lodge and Legg, held a council of war. Despite a chronic shortage of ammunition and grenades the council resolved to continue resisting until they were overrun. Sgt. Legg, as mentioned previously, volunteered with another man to attempt to reach the battalion. The men were comforted with the hope that a counter-attack might rescue them and the night slowly passed broken by odd sniping. At 7.20 a.m. it was over, quite quickly. The enemy rushed the position from three sides and 'D' Company's stand was over; the men had held the position for 22 hours and were exhausted.

Two months later, on 10th February 1918, the 13th was disbanded and the men distributed among other Essex units. The rallying cry 'Up the Hammers' would be heard no more - at least not in France.

23
The Robin Hoods
1/7th Sherwood Foresters, German Spring Offensive, 21st March 1918

The 1/7th Sherwood Foresters, a pre-war Territorial battalion raised in Nottingham, (hence the nickname) landed in France on 25th February 1915 with 1,000 officers and men. Savagely mauled at the Hohenzollern Redoubt during the Battle of Loos in 1915, the Sherwoods were heavily reinforced time and time again over the next twelve months. The unit received another draft just in time for the first day of the Battle of the Somme where the battalion lost 409 officers and other ranks out of an attacking force numbering 536. Manpower continued to drain away throughout 1917 and on 6th February 1918 the 1/7th absorbed the 2/7th battalion of their regiment. There were just eleven members left of the original 'Robin Hoods.'

When Operation Michael, the German Spring offensive, swept over the British sector on 21st March 1918 there were a number of British units which only offered a token resistance before surrendering, but the 1/7th was not one of them. The integrated battalion was manning a sector of the 59th (North Midland) Division's line, one of the fourteen Divisions of the Third Army which held a front of 28 miles from Arras southwards. There was no village or natural feature near the battalion and its position was marked by a map reference at Brigade H.Q.

In the final phase of the enemy bombardment which lasted for five minutes, from 9.35 a.m. until 9.40 a.m., a hurricane of high explosive shells delivered by every available gun and mortar blasted the British line. Under cover of this barrage German storm troops moved out and laid down in No-Man's-Land and the assaulting infantry who were to follow packed into their jump-off trenches.

Punctually at 9.40 a.m. the shelling stopped and the 1/7th was attacked along the length of its sector. The unit's history records that one of the Lewis gun teams had moved out of the trench during the enemy shelling and positioned themselves in a shell crater in No-Man's-Land. This single gun wreaked havoc on the advancing German infantry until the crew were killed and the gun destroyed by a minenwerfer bomb. Unfortunately the names of this gallant group are not known. Little is known of the actual conflict between the 1/7th and their adversaries except that it lasted just over an hour and there was murderous hand-to-hand fighting before the battalion was overwhelmed.

Two wounded officers and twelve men managed to escape before the battalion was completely surrounded. Twelve officers, 40 N.C.O.s and 119 men were killed and another twelve officers and 470 rank and file, many of them wounded, were taken prisoner. The total of 171 dead is far higher than that of any other British battalion on that day. Among the officers who were killed were eight second lieutenants, seven of whom had yet to see, and never would see, their twentieth birthdays The eighth subaltern, 2/Lieut. Wilson M.M., was a veteran who had been commissioned from the ranks. With a few exceptions the dead have no known graves and their names are commemorated on the Arras Memorial.

On 30th March a handful of survivors of the 1/7th were paraded in a village street behind the lines and inspected by King George V who congratulated them on the splendid performance of their battalion.

The 1/7th was reformed in April with a reinforcement of 700 officers and men, mostly conscripts transferred from Midland and Northern regiments; the remainder were recovered wounded. Two weeks later this patchwork battalion, cobbled together from many different units, was pushed back into the line on the Ypres front near Kemmel Hill. Here it immediately lost a third of its strength when the Germans mounted a new attack, but this time there were no more reinforcements. On 7th May 1918 the proud 1/7th was reduced to a training cadre.

Above: King George V inspecting the remnants of the Robin Hoods at Hermin after the Battle of Bullecourt.

Below: The King interrogating Pte. Denny of the Robin Hoods after the Battle of Bullecourt.

24

Diex Aïx

1st Royal Guernsey Light Infantry, Battles of the Somme, March 1918

Diex Aïx was the motto of the Royal Guernsey Militia and correctly translated it read 'With God's Help.' It was inherited by the Royal Guernsey Light Infantry and usually rendered as 'God Help Us,' especially when they reached the Western Front.

On the outbreak of war the Militia was mobilised in order to free Regular Army units of the garrison for duty overseas, although the militiamen themselves were not liable for such service. However, many individual Guernseymen joined the Navy or Army and not a few, born in Guernsey of French parents, enlisted in the French Army. In addition, 246 officers and men volunteers from the Militia, formed 'D' Company and also the battalion machine-gun section of the 6th Battalion, Royal Irish Regiment, which had been stationed in the island just prior to the war. Another draft of volunteers formed a full company in the 7th Battalion, Royal Irish Fusiliers, which also had pre-war associations with Guernsey.

In December 1916 the Conscription Act came into effect and on the 17th of that month the Militia was suspended for the duration of the war and the 1st Service Battalion of the Royal Guernsey Light Infantry was formed. The officers from the two Irish companies were transferred to the battalion and by April 1917 they were joined by 175 of their men who had been convalescing at home. After advanced infantry training in England the battalion, 1,008 all ranks, landed in France on 27th September 1917 but almost immediately lost two officers and 53 men who were posted back to the reserve battalion in Guernsey as too old, too young, or unfit for active service.

After arriving in France the battalion joined 86th Infantry Brigade part of the 29th Division of Gallipoli fame, commanded by Major General Sir Beauvoir de Lisle, another Guernseyman. Following battle inoculation the unit moved into the line where it was blooded at the Battle of Cambrai on 20th November 1917, fortunately with only light casualties, and the 29th Division, having taken all its objectives, began to consolidate a section of the line from Marcoing to Masnières. On 30th November, when the Germans counter-attacked in overwhelming force, the Guernsey battalion was waiting in the relative safety of Masnières as the 86th Brigade's reserve.

Storming through the right side of the salient, which had been created by their successful attack of 20th November, the enemy punched through the British line at Crevecoeur and started to roll it up from 29th Division's right flank. De Lisle deployed his 86th Brigade to meet the threat and the Guernseys were ordered south of the St. Quentin canal to hold Les Rues Vertes. On the maps this was shown as a village but in fact it was virtually a suburb of Masnières. Twice the untried and newly-trained Guernseymen were pushed back through the narrow lanes and twice they re-took the village in vicious hand-to-hand fighting. As the tide of battle swayed to and fro the Germans were unable to use their superior weight of artillery for fear of shelling their own men and were forced to rely on infantry and their numerous machine-guns.

569 Acting Sergeant Budden found four of these guns when he rushed forward alone over a small mound and found himself confronted by three enemy machine-guns being manhandled up the slope. A fourth gun, with its eight man crew, was already set up in position and facing him. This gun opened fire at point blank range but inexplicably missed Budden who promptly shot the gun's No.1, plus three more of the crew, and captured the other four men. Herding his prisoners in front of him he ran back to organise some bombers to attack the remaining guns. However, when he returned the other three guns had been withdrawn. He at once got the fourth German machine-gun into action against its former owners and inflicted heavy casualties on the retreating enemy. 590 Sgt. Le Poidevin was another doughty warrior who held a street barricade against enemy infantry when all his men except one were wounded or dead. After he was hit in both legs he crawled back during a brief lull in the fighting to collect reinforcements. Both he and Budden were awarded the D.C.M. and Budden was also commissioned in the field.

During the next two days the Germans launched seven separate attacks, each supported by medium artillery, and each time the attackers were beaten back and suffered heavy losses.

However, the stand of the brigade and the Guernseymen had left a 1,000 yard salient surrounded on three sides by the enemy. With insufficient troops the ground could not be held and the Division was ordered to fall back and straighten the line. The battalion had lost nine officers and 280 rank and file killed or wounded, and two officers and 214 other ranks missing. Many of the missing were subsequently reported as killed.

The battalion was now so weakened that it was in danger of being disbanded but by the end of the year nearly 400 men had been transferred in, which included a large draft from the North Staffordshire Regiment. There were even some horsemen from the Army Remount Service. On 18th January 1918 the reconstituted battalion was back in the line just beyond Ypres for the usual cycle of trench warfare and the attendant cycle of casualties. However, there were more reinforcements including the 65 survivors of the Guernsey companies of the 6th Royal Irish Regiment and the 7th Royal Irish Fusiliers who were transferred to their home regiment following the disbandment of the two Irish

Right: Royal Guernsey Light Infantry at Doulieu, 10th-14th April 1918.

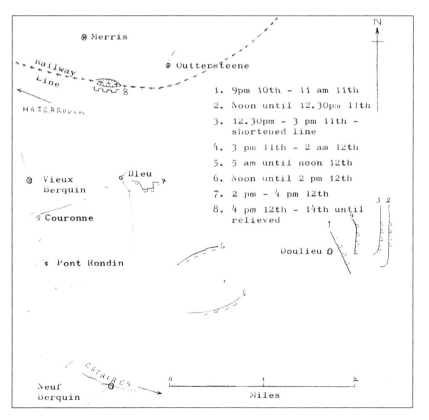

1. 9pm 10th – 11 am 11th
2. Noon until 12.30pm 11th
3. 12.30pm – 3 pm 11th – shortened line
4. 3 pm 11th – 2 am 12th
5. 5 am until noon 12th
6. Noon until 2 pm 12th
7. 2 pm – 4 pm 12th
8. 4 pm 12th – 14th until relieved

battalions. Numerous trench raids were a feature of the sector, and in one of these affairs at the end of March the battalion lost 77 men, killed, wounded or gassed.

On 21st March 1918 the Germans launched their major Spring offensive and the 29th Division was pulled out of the line and lorried to the Lys sector, south of Bailleul in Northern France, where the enemy had brushed aside a raw Portuguese division and were racing towards a vital railhead at Hazebrouck. The 86th and 87th Infantry Brigades were deployed to stem the advance. The Guernseymen moved by lorry and by foot to a position about 1,000 yards west of the village of Neuf Berquin where they arrived at 6 a.m. on 10th April and waited there for orders. Intelligence officers reported that the situation was 'fluid' - in layman's language this meant that nobody knew what was happening - other than the Germans.

At 5.30 p.m. the battalion was ordered to march to Doulieu, four miles to the north-east, and dig in east of the village. The next morning the Guernseymen left their newly dug trenches and were on the move once more in order to plug a mile long gap between the 87th Brigade and the 40th Division on the left. As

Above: German prisoners of war dismantling a British-built loop-holed street barricade in Arras on 29th April 1918. In fact these barricades had not been needed as the German Spring Offensive stopped short just to the east of Arras. The Germans belong to the 141 Infantry Regiment, 35th Division; note the musician's 'Wings' on the man third from the left (Imperial War Museum)

they were hurried forward they came under heavy machine-gun fire and by early afternoon 'B' and 'C' Companies had been practically wiped out. 'A' and 'D' Companies with Battalion Headquarters held a shortened line until 3 p.m. when they were forced to fall back a few hundred yards with instructions to dig in just east of Doulieu.

The Lys offensive in which the battalion was now heavily involved was the second and smaller phase, codenamed 'Georgette,' of the German main onslaught which had smashed through the British positions on the Somme.

Doulieu was by-passed by the enemy and at 2 a.m. on 12th April the Guernseys were ordered to fall back and dig in again facing south. They held this position until noon when they were again outflanked and the battalion, or what was left of it, withdrew another 1,000 yards to dig in for the fourth time. Casualties by now had reduced the battalion strength to that of a company. This position was held for barely two hours when a further retreat was made to the hamlet of Bleu where the surviving Guernseymen lined the bank of a small stream. Blasted out of there by heavy artillery fire the men fell back to a cutting on the Hazebrouck-Bailleul railway line. Here the new front line was finally stabilised and the Guernseys held on against fresh enemy attacks until they were relieved by Australian troops early on 14th April.

The C.O., Lieut. Colonel de Havilland, brought out just three officers and 55 other ranks, although another 47 who had become detached during the running battle, and had fought alongside other units, joined later. Some of the Channel Islands families suffered grievous losses; Private James Guille, who hailed from Sark, joined his four brothers and cousins who had already been killed in action with the battalion. Five of the Gallienne clan were also among the dead, the last of them, Private Harold Gallienne, killed on 13th April. The two D.C.M. winners from Cambrai, Budden and Le Poidevin, were both convalescent in England and thus fortunately missed the finale at the Lys.

Field Marshal Haig's despatch of 20th July 1918 particularly mentioned the 'gallant service' of the Guernseys for their part in the fighting near Doulieu, but as a fighting unit the 1st Battalion was finished. On 27th April, a bare seven months after arriving in France, the shattered remnants took over from the Honourable Artillery Company as guard troops at Haig's G.H.Q. in Montreuil.

25
Manchester Hill
16th Manchesters, Battle of
St. Quentin, 21st March 1918

Men of the 16th (Service) Battalion, Manchester Regiment, better known as the 1st Manchester Pals, one of 'Kitchener's mob,' received their baptism of fire on 7th December 1915 at Hebuterne. However, it was not until 1st July 1916 that they went over the top in their first major battle on the Somme. Part of the 90th Infantry Brigade of the 30th Division they were on the extreme right of the British line and the Pals acquitted themselves well, taking all their objectives and capturing two field guns. Although only two officers and 92 men had been killed, a light bill when compared with the murderous casualties suffered by some of the other battalions, virtually all the officers and over 300 men had been wounded.

Strengthened by drafts from 22 different units, including cavalry and Corps as well as infantry, the 16th was again in action at Guillemont on 30th July but the British attackers were repelled and the 16th lost seven officers killed and over 200 other ranks killed, wounded or missing. Throughout 1917 at Messines and Wytschaete, and during the Third Battle of Ypres, the familiar cycle of casualties replaced by reinforcements which, in turn, became casualties, was repeated time and time again. Finally, at the beginning of 1918, the Pals were withdrawn to the St. Quentin sector where they received a large draft from the recently disbanded 7th East Surreys plus 13 officers and 280 other ranks from their own 19th Manchesters, also disbanded.

Following the mutiny by regiments of the French Army in 1917, the British battle line now stretched about 50 miles from the Scarpe to the Oise and was held by 24 Divisions. The Germans, freed from the necessity to fight on two fronts after the collapse of Russia, were able to field some 60 Divisions with another 30 in immediate reserve. Furthermore, the enemy weight, and concentration, of artillery was much greater than that of the British. A Forward Zone in front of the British lines held a number of redoubts, usually manned at battalion strength, which were expected to hold out for at least 48 hours and inflict maximum casualties and delay on an attacking enemy. A German push, with the intention of breaking through to the Channel ports, was known to be imminent. The 16th moved into one of these redoubts, promptly dubbed Manchester Hill, on 18th March just in time for the threatened German Spring Offensive.

Manchester Hill covered the main battle position held by the Brigade around Savy and also controlled the important St. Quentin-Savy road. Although in reality the redoubt was situated on rising ground rather than a hill it still commanded an excellent field fire in every direction. It was backed by a quarry on its reverse slope which gave good cover and was provided with mortar emplacements and dugouts. On either side of the strongpoint minor valleys and depressions in the terrain were dominated by carefully sited machine-guns. Thus the redoubt was a tactical feature of great strength and the location of its posts, the interlocking patterns of cross fire, and triple belts of barbed wire made it almost impregnable - on a clear day. 'A' Company supported by 'C' Company held the right front and 'B' Company plus two platoons from 'C' were on the left. The actual redoubt was garrisoned by 'D' Company and, initially, Battalion H.Q. was situated on the southern slope of the quarry.

On the night of 20/21st March the commanding officer of the 1st Pals, Lieut. Colonel Elstob D.S.O., M.C., the only officer left out of those who had landed in France back in November 1915, made the rounds of his posts impressing on his men that they were to fight to the last round should the German attack materi-alise. All was quiet until 6.30 a.m. when a massive bombardment of high explosive, shrapnel and gas shells began to batter British positions all along the line. What is more, the smoke of bursting missiles thickened the already dense fog which had descended just before dawn. Nothing could have been more disastrous; visi-bility was reduced to a few feet, the advantage of defence in depth was negated and the carefully sited heavy machine-guns were almost useless. At 7.30 a.m. the C.O. and H.Q. Company moved from the quarry to battle headquarters on Manchester Hill and shortly after 8 a.m. the barrage intensified and telephone wires to the supporting company were cut. At about 8.30 a.m. the first information of the enemy infantry came when a runner struggled through to Battalion H.Q. with the news that 'A' Company had been overwhelmed and this was followed a few minutes later with similar bad news from 'B' and 'C' Companies.

Then followed a lull with some desultory firing but the German storm troops were under orders to infiltrate the British main battle line and leave any defended positions to the infantry. The first indication of German troops in the redoubt proper was a scream from a sentry in one of the outer posts who had just been bayoneted. Manchester Hill was now surrounded by German infantry and the left and right forward posts on the redoubt were heavily engaged, but the enemy attacks were not pressed fully home. By noon the fog had lifted and the garrison was heartened by the sight of a British relief column marching down the road towards them from the battle zone. Alas, it transpired that the huge formation was composed of British prisoners under escort and the Manchesters realised just how far the enemy had advanced. By 2 p.m. the enemy were attacking in force and many of the defenders had been killed or wounded. Learning that German infantry had entered the redoubt from the south the C.O. personally erected a bombing block between his opponents and the H.Q. dugout. Although shot at and bombed he accounted single-handed for the German bombing party and when his revolver ammunition was exhausted he continued to hold the block using Mills bombs. The enemy subsequently abandoned the idea of storming the bombing block from the front and swarmed over the top of the trench in large numbers. Col. Elstob armed himself with a rifle and played his part in disposing of this fresh wave of assailants. Here he was wounded for the first time but returned after his wound had been dressed by Corporal Stenson, the medical N.C.O. Stenson showed great courage throughout the day in attending to the wounded, despite the fact that he had been badly wounded himself in the early stages of the attack.

6630 Sergeant Hoye, a regular soldier and the Lewis gun N.C.O., was another stalwart in the defence of the redoubt. Together with two young soldiers he held a post on the western edge of the quarry until the enemy were upon him, and while changing a pan on the gun he and his companions were shot and killed.

The Germans now made a determined attack in force and also brought up several field guns whose crews, firing over open sights, destroyed the remaining British heavy machine-guns. Meanwhile Col. Elstob had been wounded for the third time. He refused a call to surrender but as he climbed onto a fire step to throw a grenade he was shot and fell forward; his adjutant, Captain Sharples reached up to pull him back and he too was shot and killed. The end was now in sight and about 3.20 p.m. the redoubt fell.

Captain Walker R.A.M.C., the medical officer, was another hero who had behaved fearlessly throughout the day. When the enemy finally rushed the quarry it was due to Capt. Walker's courage that they did not blow up the battalion aid post. While they were actually throwing bombs down the entrance, the M.O. dashed up the dugout steps at great personal risk of meeting a grenade on the way, or a bullet or bayonet at the top, and convinced the Germans that the dugout was a Red Cross station. Of the original redoubt garrison of eight officers and 160 other ranks only two officers and 15 men survived.

One of the Manchesters killed in the redoubt was 44112 Private Herman Schaefer, born in Manchester of German parents and one of that city's large pre-war German population. His cousin, 6802 Carl Schaefer, had been a regular soldier and a lance sergeant in the 16th when he was killed in action at Guillemont in July 1917. Another Schaefer cousin was on holiday from his Manchester mill and in the Fatherland when war was declared and he found himself conscripted into the German Army. The stormers of the redoubt were drawn from the 2nd Battalion, 158th Infantry Regiment, commanded by Hauptmann Gabeke who survived the First World War but not the Second. He was killed fighting on the Russian Front in 1942.

The only member of the 16th to be decorated for the defence of Manchester Hill was the C.O., Wilfrith Elstob the former schoolmaster. His Victoria Cross was gazetted on 9th June 1919. 'For most conspicuous bravery, devotion to duty and self-sacrifice at Manchester Redoubt, near St. Quentin, on the 21st March 1918. During the preliminary bombardment he encouraged his men in the posts in the Redoubt by frequent visits and when repeated attacks developed controlled the defence at the points threatened, giving personal support with revolver, rifle and bombs. Single handed he repulsed one bombing assault, driving back the enemy and inflicting severe casualties. Later when ammunition was required he made several journeys under severe fire in order to replenish supply.

Throughout the day Lt. Col. Elstob, although twice wounded, showed the most fearless disregard of his own safety, and by his encouragement and noble example inspired his command to the

Left: Lt.-Col. Wilfrith Elstob V.C., D.S.O., M.C.

full degree. The Manchester Redoubt was surrounded in the first wave of the enemy attack, but by means of buried cable Lt. Col. Elstob was able to assure his Brigade Commander "That the Manchester Regiment will defend Manchester Hill to the last."

Some time after, the post was overcome by vastly superior forces and this very gallant officer was killed in the final assault, having maintained to the end the duty which he impressed on his men, namely "Here we fight and here we die." He set the highest example of valour, determination, endurance and fine soldierly bearing.'

The 16th was reduced to a training cadre on 13th May 1918 and assisted with battle inoculation for various units of the newly landed U.S. Army. The party returned to England on 18th June for the battalion to be reconstituted from drafts and recovered wounded. The reformed 16th returned to France on 4th June 1918.

26
No Retreat and No Surrender
4th Grenadier Guards, Battle of Hazebrouck, 13th April 1918

No doubt H.M.'s First Foot Guards, the Grenadiers, who tend to refer to Line Regiments as 'The Feet,' might be put out to find themselves in a book devoted to the P.B.I. Nevertheless, guardsmen are foot soldiers (and very good ones too) armed with a rifle and bayonet, just like the infantry.

The 4th Battalion, Grenadier Guards, landed in France on 19th August 1915, and joined the newly-formed Guards Division in nice time for the Battle of Loos. This offensive opened on 25th September 1915 and, by the 29th, had cost the battalion 11 officers and 342 other ranks killed, wounded and gassed. In between tours of duty in the trenches, training and 'resting,' the 4th was heavily engaged in some of the later battles on the Somme, notably the storming of Lesboeufs and Morval. As a result, between 18th and 26th September 1916, unit casualties totalled 11 officers and 445 rank and file. The battalion's next major action was helping to stem the German counter-attack at Cambrai in November 1917.

On 9th April 1918, in the aftermath of the German Spring offensive, the enemy opened a concentrated attack and hurled nine Divisions against the British/Portuguese front between Armentières and La Bassée. Smashing through the Portuguese sector the German troops punched forward in the hope of gaining the Channel ports or, at least, cutting the Allied communications, with all that this would entail. The British XV Corps had been driven back to a line between Vieux Berquin and a point west of Merville, south-east of Hazebrouck, but the enemy having captured Neuf Berquin and advanced on Vierhoek, were poised for another vital breakthrough. The situation was now critical.

Such was the state of affairs on 12th April when the 4th Guards Brigade was ordered forward to take Vierhoek, Pont Rondin and Les Puresbecques, and restore contact with the 29th Division last reported in the vicinity of Vieux Berquin.

However, before the Guards could make much headway they were vigorously attacked and held by strong German forces. It was now essential to hold the line until the Australian Division, being rushed up from the rear, could detrain and establish defensive positions. In view of the gravity of the situation General de Lisle, commanding XV Corps, issued an order that no retirement would be made without an order in writing, signed by a responsible officer, who must be prepared to justify his action before a court martial. In the meantime, until reinforcements arrived, every inch of ground must be disputed and every man must stand firm.

The Guards were in position by dawn but as soon as it was light a German barrage swept the front and minenwerfers and machine-guns opened up whenever their crews detected movement in the British lines. Despite the bombardment the 3rd Coldstream Guards was ordered to move forward and deny the enemy movement on the Merville-Neuf Berquin road while from the 4th Grenadiers, No.1 Company was to seize Vierhoek, and Captain Pryce with two platoons from No.2 Company was to occupy Point Rondin. The operation was timed for 11 a.m. but the Coldstreamers encountered such strenuous opposition that they were unable to advance more than 100 yards. Similarly, the platoons from No.1 Company of the 4th Grenadiers were unable to make headway towards Vierhoek owing to intense and accurate artillery and machine-gun fire, and they suffered severely in the attempt. The only success was that of No.2 Company which made a skilful advance towards Pont Rondin, led by Captain Pryce himself. Houses on the approach to the objective were occupied by Germans with Bergmann light machine-guns and these had to be cleared. No.2 Company worked systematically from house to house silencing the guns and killing 30 Germans. The guns were taken together with some prisoners. During the entire operation the guardsmen were under heavy fire, not only from machine-guns but also a battery of field guns which were firing over open sights from a position some 300 yards down the road.

By 3 p.m. the situation was very critical. The Coldstreams reported that there was no sign of the 50th Division, which should have been on their right flank, and Capt. Pryce sent word that his left flank was in the air and Germans could be seen 1,000 yards in rear of his men. Affairs on the right improved when a company of the Irish Guards counter-attacked in conjunction with a company of Coldstreamers, but there were no extra troops available for the left flank. Accordingly, Capt. Pryce was ordered to fall back, in order to maintain contact with the rest of the battalion, and having reached the position indicated he held on in spite of several determined attacks by the enemy.

About 4.30 p.m. the C.O. visited the left of the line and found No.2 Company rather scattered as it had been obliged to also form a defensive flank. When night fell the 4th Battalion front was still intact, but at a heavy cost in men. Capt. Pryce's No.2 Company had lost an officer and 80 men out of the three officers and 120 rank and file who went into action that morning, and No.4 Company was minus 70% of its strength, including all the officers. Total casualties in the battalion were very heavy, but on the other hand the ground in front of the battalion was literally piled with enemy dead; the 4th had fired off no less than 70,000 rounds of ammunition.

During the night of the 12/13th April, 4th Guards Brigade was ordered to shorten the line and the 4th Battalion's new front extended south from La Couronne. This new frontage was 1,800 yards long and facing flat country with not even one hedge to mask the newly dug trenches. So heavily had the Battalion suffered that it could only field nine officers and 180 other ranks, or in other words one man to every ten yards of front.

Dawn on the 13th brought thick fog (the Germans were usually lucky with their weather) in which the enemy were able to move machine-guns close to the British line. As soon as the mist cleared away the Germans laid down a barrage with these machine-guns and, under cover of this fire, crawled forward in ones and twos and established sniping posts close to the Guards' trenches. Strong enemy attacks developed all along the line and the C.O. reminded his company commanders that they must fight to the end. About 12.30 p.m. the 12th Pioneer Battalion of the K.O.Y.L.I. at La Couronne was practically blown out of its trenches by massed enemy mortars and German infantry took the opportunity to work round to the rear of them. The survivors of the 12th Pioneers had no choice but to retire and this left the left flank of the 4th Battalion in the air, yet again.

Captain Pryce now sent an urgent message that the Germans were in Vieux Berquin and La Couronne and a column, estimated to be the strength of two battalions, was advancing from Bleu. He added that he was not strong enough in manpower to resist much longer the repeated assaults of so

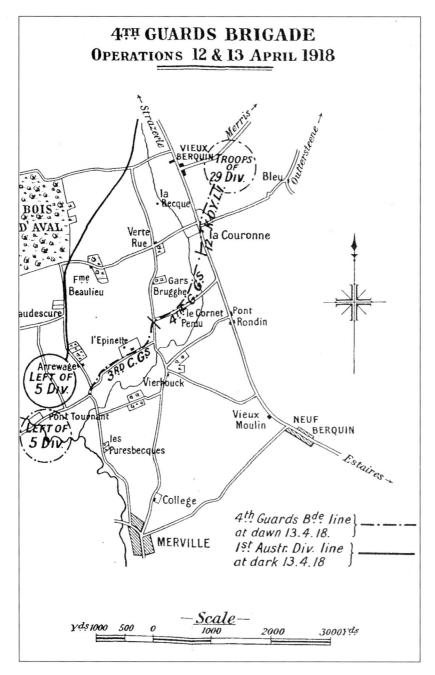

4TH GUARDS BRIGADE
OPERATIONS 12 & 13 APRIL 1918

large a force. A company of the Irish Guards was despatched to
Pryce's position, but it never reached him. Moving north of the
road leading to La Couronne the Irishmen collided with a large
formation of Germans coming from La Beque. The Irish were

unable to fight their way through the opposition and only a sergeant and six men escaped.

Back in No.2 Company's trenches an attempt was made to shift the remaining Lewis gun to afford a better field of fire, but as soon as they moved the crew were struck down and the gun wrecked by minenwerfer bombs. The machine-gun officer, 2/Lieut. Phillips, tried to rejoin the main party but was hit in the thigh and disabled. No.2 Company was now reduced to 30 men who, standing back-to-back for they were also being assailed from the rear, continued to beat off their opponents throughout the day with rapid and deadly rifle fire. But by evening the defenders were practically at the end of their tether; only 18 men, some of them wounded, were left on their feet and every round of ammunition had been expended.

It was now 8.15 p.m. and the absence of any shots encouraged a party of German infantry to press forward to within 80 yards of the stubbornly held trenches. Although the Guards had fired their last cartridge they still had their bayonets and Pryce ordered the men to fix bayonets and charge. Charge they did, straight at the advancing enemy who were unable to fire for fear of hitting their own men in rear of the Grenadiers. The adventurous Germans fled and Pryce took his men, now numbering 14, back to the trench, but the enemy had seen the incredible weakness of their adversaries.

Below: Captain Thomas Tannatt Pryce V.C., M.C.

Full of confidence the Germans came on once more and once more Captain Pryce led the tattered remnants of his company in their final bayonet charge. When last seen they were still fighting it out with cold steel and ignoring demands to surrender.

Survivors of the 4th Battalion managed to make their way back to the Australian line which by now had been established. Of the 19 officers who had gone into action only two were left and total casualties amongst other ranks were 504, or 90% of the battalion strength.

Pryce was awarded a posthumous Victoria Cross and his citation, published in the *London Gazette* of 22nd May 1918 reads: 'Lieutenant (A/Capt.) Thomas Tannatt Pryce, M.C., G. Gds. For most conspicuous bravery, devotion to duty, and self-sacrifice in command of a flank on the left of the Grenadier Guards.

Having been ordered to attack a village, he personally led forward two platoons, working from house to house, killing some thirty of the enemy, seven of whom he killed himself.

The next day he was occupying a position with some thirty to forty men, the remainder of his company having become casualties. As early as 8.15 a.m. his left flank was surrounded and the enemy was enfilading him.

He was attacked no less than four times during the day, and each time beat off the hostile attack, killing many of the enemy. Meanwhile the enemy brought up three field guns to within 300 yards of his line, and were firing over open sights and knocking his trench in. At 6.15 p.m. the enemy had worked to within sixty yards of his trench. He then called on his men, telling them to cheer and charge the enemy and fight to the last. Led by Captain Pryce, they left their trench and drove back the enemy, with the bayonet, some 100 yards. Half an hour later the enemy had again approached in stronger force. By this time Captain Pryce had only 17 men left, and every round of his ammunition had been fired. Determined that there should be no surrender, he once again led his men forward in a bayonet charge, and was last seen engaged in a fierce hand-to-hand struggle with overwhelming numbers of the enemy.

With some forty men he had held back at least one enemy battalion for over ten hours. His company undoubtedly stopped the advance through the British line, and thus had great influence on the battle.'

Pryce, age 32, entered the Guards by a circuitous route. Married, with three young daughters, he enlisted in the Honourable Artillery Company on the outbreak of war and fought with that regiment in France in 1914. Commissioned into the Gloucestershire Regiment in 1915 he was wounded, and won the M.C. at Gommecourt. After convalescence in England he returned to the Western Front in May 1916 and, shortly afterwards, was again wounded and awarded a bar to his Military Cross. He transferred to the Grenadier Guards later in 1916 and joined the 4th battalion of his regiment, with a draft, in February 1917.

Captain Pryce has no known grave and his name is commemorated, with many others, on the Ploegsteert Memorial in Belgium.

27
In Ungrudging Sacrifice
2nd Devons, Bois des Buttes, Battle of the Aisne, 27th May 1918

On the outbreak of World War I the 2nd Battalion, Devonshire Regiment, was stationed in Egypt and did not land in France until 5th November 1914. Thus the Devons missed Mons, Le Cateau, the Marne and the earlier battles of Ypres which destroyed so much of the British regular army. Nevertheless, the last six weeks fighting of 1914 cost the battalion six officers and 82 other ranks dead, and treble that number wounded. Throughout 1915 and the first months of 1916 the 2nd Devons endured the grinding misery of trench warfare and its attendant list of casualties. This was to change (or so they were told) on 1st July 1916 when the bulk of Kitchener's volunteers would smash their way through the German barbed wire on the Somme. There would be nothing to stop them as the enemy trenches and defenders were to be pulverised by British artillery.

The battalion played host to four pairs of brothers, although two of those pairs had already been separated when Bert Kingdom and Fred Drew had died at Neuve Chapelle on 10th March 1915. Now Lance Corporal Gordon Kingdom and the surviving Drew boy were hoping for better luck in the forthcoming battle which, according to the brass, would merely be a case of rounding up the demoralised enemy infantry. There were also the Farley brothers who were true sons of Devon, both of them born in Kennford. 8871 Pte. George Farley, a pre-war regular, had promised his widowed mother that he would keep an eye on his younger brother Fred, one of Kitchener's mob. Brin and George Davies, the fourth pair of brothers, were also Kitchener's men and this would be their first big engagement.

On 1st July the 2nd Devons formed part of the 23rd Infantry Brigade of the 8th Division, whose objective was to attack the Ovillers spur, advance along Mash Valley, and take Pozières, which was just in front of the German second line. At 7.30 a.m. as the British barrage lifted from the enemy's front positions and onto his support trenches the 2nd Devons in extended line advanced into No-Man's-Land. The next wave of troops filing into the jump-off trenches looked over the parapet and saw the leading files of Devons lying out in No-Man's-Land waiting, as the onlookers thought, for a chance to move forward. But the inert bodies they saw were the dead, dying and wounded, 443 officers and men to be precise, scythed down by untouched German machine-guns. There would be no more brothers in the battalion; L/Cpl. Kingdom, the remaining Drew and both Davies boys were among the dead. The two Farley brothers were side by side as they went over the top - and side by side as they died.

For the rest of the year, and throughout 1917 and into 1918, the story of the 2nd Devons repeated the pattern endured by so many of the infantry units on the Western Front - a never-ending cycle of casualties replaced by inexperienced recruits and recovered wounded. When the German Spring Offensive broke on 21st March 1918 the 23rd Brigade, which comprised the 2nd Middlesex and 2nd West Yorks, as well as the Devons, was rushed into the line to hold the west bank of the Somme. The sector allocated to the men from Devon ran from south of Happlincourt to the bridge near St. Christ, which the engineers were preparing to blow. Given the task of holding the bridge the battalion was deployed to take advantage of the little cover available.

Three times that night the Germans attempted to storm the bridge and on each occasion were driven back in brutal hand-to-hand fighting. The next morning, Palm Sunday, was fairly quiet apart from a number of enemy howitzers which hammered the British positions at close range. There was a brilliantly fine dawn on Monday, 25th March and the countryside looked delightful; and a striking contrast to the blood stained swamps of the Ypres salient. But the weather was the only item of good news. The Germans had crossed the river upstream at Eterpigny and, having driven in the West Yorkshires, were in the process of surrounding the 2nd Middlesex, on the left flank of the Devons. In addition, the enemy had broken through on the right and were threatening to take the Devons in the rear.

Ordered to retire, the battalion made a fighting withdrawal, company by company, with every man who could hold a rifle, which included cooks, batmen and clerks, thrown into the fighting line. The retreat continued until the German advance ground to a halt short of Amiens. On 22nd March the Devons had gone into action mustering 25 officers and 900 other ranks. On 2nd April the number had been reduced to ten officers and 300 men.

Taken out of the line the survivors were rested and reinforced. 'Rested' was synonymous with drills, polishing brasses and humping supplies while the reinforcements, apart from a few recovered wounded, were recruits whose scrappy training back in England had not included firing their newly issued rifles.

On 12th May the 2nd Devons were moved to a peaceful sector on the Aisne to which tired French Divisions were normally sent to recuperate. The 23rd Brigade occupied a frontage of nearly 10,000 yards from Berry au Bac to mid-way between Juvincourt and Corbeny. This stretch would normally have demanded nine battalions but British commanders were assured that the area was so quiet that even when troops were in the line it would be easy to give the young soldiers the training they so badly needed. The battalion was now well up to strength in officers as no fewer than 28 had been posted in during the past few weeks although not all of them were infantrymen; several were captains transferred from the Army Service Corps. However, the number of other ranks was still well below establishment and only totalled about 650.

About 4 p.m. information was received that a German attack was impending and the battalion, nominally in reserve, was established in underground bunkers at the Bois des Buttes. This was a small hill, with two separate summits, standing immediately in front of Juvincourt and about three quarters of a mile behind the front line. The West Yorkshires were holding the forward area behind the front line and the Middlesex men were in the battle zone behind the Yorks. Low brushwood covered the summits of the hill and in many places the grass and herbage was high enough to cover the barbed wire entanglements. In addition, the so-called trenches in front of the hills were badly maintained and sited with poor fields of fire to the front. The area had been previously occupied by the French whose gun sites, unknown to the British, had not been changed for a whole year. Hence the German artillery spotters had taken the opportunity to register and range on every emplacement. These were now occupied by British batteries which had not yet been given the opportunity to re-locate their guns.

At 1 o'clock in the morning on 27th May 1918 the ground shook as 2,000 enemy guns open fire, saturating the British

161

gun sites and the Bois des Buttes. Many of the British field guns and their crews were destroyed in the first hour or so and the infantry, crouching in their dugouts and waiting for the order to move out wondered why there was so little counter-battery fire coming from their own side. The barrage now included gas shells as well as high explosive and the Devon commanding officer, Lieut. Colonel Anderson-Morshead, waited in vain for information on any enemy movement from the front or Brigade H.Q. All the telephone lines were cut and runners, sent out in spaced pairs, failed to survive the hurricane of shell fire.

Accordingly, at first light the C.O. decided to wait no longer but ordered his men out of their dugouts, those that had not been entombed alive, to their battle stations in the trenches.

'B' Company led by Lieut. Oreton was on the extreme left, facing Laon, with the 50th Division on its left and 'C' and 'D' Companies commanded respectively by Lieuts. Tindall and Harris, were positioned as near to the wood as they could manage and were more or less astride the road; 'C' Company on the right and 'D' on the left. 'A' Company and Battalion Head-quarters occupied the trench round the sides of the hills which contained the shelters.

Shells continued to rain down as the wounded tried to make their way back to the regimental aid post only a few yards to the rear but few of them got that far. Furthermore, every dawn on this front had been crystal clear but, with the luck of the Germans, this particular morning heralded a hanging white haze thickened by dust and the smoke of exploding shells. It was practically impossible to see anything beyond a few yards. Unbeknown to the Devons not only had the front given way but German infantry had also penetrated British positions on the Devons' right and also broken through the 50th Division lines on their left. It was now about 5 a.m. and the attackers had over-run the West Yorks. and were through the battle zone, despite all the efforts of the heavily out-numbered Middlesex.

'B' Company was the first to be engaged by long lines of enemy infantry, preceded by storm troops looming up out of the mist, and the unusual spectacle of two enemy tanks lumbering towards them each fitted with a cable from which flew a captive observation balloon. As the mist began to lift German aero-planes were not only machine-gunning the defenders but also spotting for the enemy artillery and the shelling, which had lifted onto the rear areas, was now redirected back onto the

Devons. Looking to the right, stragglers from other regiments could be seen making for the rear as fast as their exhausted state would allow. A Devon corporal was sent over to them with an invitation to join the Devons but the offer was declined and the only thing they wished to join was a general exodus away from German flame-throwers and tanks.

The remainder of the battalion were now heavily engaged and although they held their immediate assailants at bay hordes of enemy troops began to appear on the left flank, and rear, and at about 7 a.m. the direct line of retreat was cut. All across the sector isolated groups and platoons fought on, deceiving their attackers that the defenders were much more numerous than had been supposed.

Lieut. Tindall and most of his men were killed when he, and the survivors of 'C' Company, fixed bayonets and charged head-long into a German formation estimated at battalion strength. 'D' Company was forced back leaving behind its company commander, Lieut. Harris of the 2nd Rhodesian Regiment, attached to the South Staffs but seconded to the Devons, who was severely wounded and presumed to be dead. He recovered consciousness a week later as a prisoner of war in Germany. His

Below: The Last Stand of the 2nd Devons at Bois-des-Buttes, 27th May 1918 by Captain W.B.Wollen.

second in command, 2/Lieut. Pells, whose only child was drowned when the *Lusitania* was torpedoed by U-20 and sunk, equipped himself with a spare rifle and continued to kill Germans until he himself was killed. At about this time the C.O. issued written orders that there was to be no retreat and the Devons must hold their ground at all costs. However, this message did not reach all the men, some of whom were split up in a maze of old trenches. Numbers 5 and 6 Platoons for example became separated from the main body and made three attempts each in a different direction, to break out. Eventually No.6 Platoon led by 2/Lieut. Clarke managed to reach the bridge and win free. The men of No.5 Platoon under 2/Lieut. Hill were not so fortunate. They were caught by machine-gun fire while trying to make a stand but were finally cornered near the river. By that time only the officer and four men, all out of ammunition, remained to be captured.

A stubborn resistance was still being offered in the support company's position where the colonel and his adjutant, Captain Burke, had rallied the survivors, together with a few men who had fallen back from the front line. About 9.30 a.m., almost out of ammunition, these two officers with less than 50 men charged down the hill and opened fire on some German artillery teams coming up the hill from Juvincourt. At this point Col. Anderson-Morshead was killed by a sniper. Capt. Burke with the survivors of the charge, about 20 all told, went back half-way up the hill which afforded a better field of fire. They held out for a little while having taken ammunition from the pouches of the dead but this soon ran out, and as they prepared for a final suicidal charge Burke was seriously wounded and the party was overwhelmed.

Very few of the battalion escaped. Many had been killed in the area of Bois des Buttes and the majority of those who attempted to break out had been killed or captured. Only 2/Lieut. Clarke's group, plus some stragglers and a few men who managed to swim the river, were finally collected as the nucleus for a stand south of Pontavert. Twenty-three officers and 528 other ranks were killed, wounded or missing. The survivors, who became part of a composite battalion of odds and sods were still fighting four days later until the German advance had been halted. None of the officers and men involved was decorated for their part in the battalion's magnificent last ditch stand. However, a few weeks later, the action was the subject of IX Corps Special

Order No.4 dated 11th July 1918, headed '2nd Battalion The Devonshire Regiment - In commemoration of its exploits at Bois des Buttes on the Aisne on 27th May 1918.' The Order read, 'A Battery Commander who was on the spot states that at a late hour in the morning he found the Commanding Officer of the Second Devonshire Regiment and a handful of men holding on to the last trench north of the Aisne. They were in a position where they were entirely without hope of help, but were fighting on grimly. The Commanding Officer himself was calmly writing his orders with a storm of H.E. shell falling round him. His magnificent bearing, dauntless courage and determination to carry on to the end were worthy of the best admiration. There is no doubt that this Battalion perished en masse. It refused to surrender and fought to the last.

The officer commanding the 2nd Devonshire Regiment (Lt. Col. P.R. Anderson-Morshead) together with 28 other officers and 552 other ranks, practically the whole Battalion in the area north of the River Aisne, fought it out to the last as ordered - a glorious record.' The Order was signed by Major B. L. Montgomery (the future Field Marshal).

On 21st August 1918 General Order No.371 from the French Fifth Army carried the citation for the award of the Croix de Guerre avec Palme to the 2nd Devons. An abbreviated translation reads: 'On 27th May 1918 north of the Aisne at a time when the British trenches were being subjected to fierce attacks the 2nd Battalion The Devonshire Regiment repelled successive enemy assaults with gallantry and determination and maintained an unbroken front till a late hour. Inspired by the sangfroid of their gallant commander... the few survivors held on to their trenches and fought to the last with an unhesitating obedience to orders. The staunchness of this Battalion permitted the defences south of the Aisne to be completed.

Thus the whole Battalion, 28 officers and 552 non-commissioned officers and men responded with one accord and offered their lives in ungrudging sacrifice to the sacred cause of the Allies.' (it will be noticed that the casualty figures differ slightly from those given in the regimental history).

The presentation of the medal was performed by General de Laguishe in France at a ceremonial parade of the 8th Division on 5th December 1918. The cross was pinned to the camp flag and both medal and flag are now in the National Army Museum in London.

28

Land-Locked Sailors

The Royal Naval Division on Four Fronts, 1914–1918

Just over 40% of the Royal Navy's casualties from 1914 to 1918 were suffered by sailors and marines who never served at sea, but still managed to win over 1,000 awards for gallantry including Victoria Crosses and an Albert Medal. In 1914, following the mobilisation of the Royal Fleet Reserve, Royal Naval Reserve and the Royal Navy Volunteer Reserve, the Admiralty, probably for the first time in its history, had more men than were required for sea service. In addition, the War Office was swamped with Kitchener's men, many of whom they were unable to feed or clothe, and a large number of these (mostly North Countrymen) were willingly handed over to the Admiralty. Hence the Royal Naval Division, composed of seamen, marines and Kitchener's volunteers, came into being to fight in an infantry role, as a temporary measure, until such time as they were needed afloat. That time never arrived and the sailors turned soldiers were to fight on throughout the Great War and earn a reputation as a fighting force second to none.

The Division consisted of three brigades, two of which were naval and the third manned by Royal Marines. The 1st Brigade consisted of the Collingwood, Hawke, Benbow and Drake Battalions; the 2nd comprised the Howe, Hood, Anson and Nelson Battalions, while four Royal Marine Light Infantry battalions titled Portsmouth, Plymouth, Chatham and R.M. Artillery (the latter was withdrawn in September 1914 and replaced by the Deal Battalion) constituted the 3rd Brigade. Training was still in progress when, on 2nd October 1914, the Germans broke through the outer line of the Antwerp forts and drove the Belgian Field Army back on the line of the Grand Nethe. This left the fortress troops unsupported and the R.N.D. was despatched to bolster the sagging Belgian defences. First into action were the Royal Marine battalions which detrained at Edeghen about four miles south of Antwerp on 4th October and

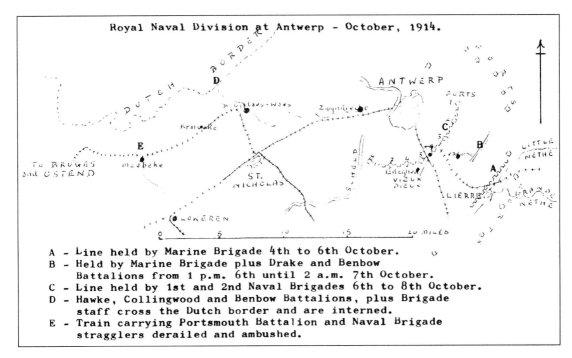

Royal Naval Division at Antwerp - October, 1914.

A – Line held by Marine Brigade 4th to 6th October.
B – Held by Marine Brigade plus Drake and Benbow
    Battalions from 1 p.m. 6th until 2 a.m. 7th October.
C – Line held by 1st and 2nd Naval Brigades 6th to 8th October.
D – Hawke, Collingwood and Benbow Battalions, plus Brigade
    staff cross the Dutch border and are interned.
E – Train carrying Portsmouth Battalion and Naval Brigade
    stragglers derailed and ambushed.

Above: Royal Naval Division at Antwerp, October 1914.

later that morning moved into trenches on the western bank of the Little Nethe, north of Lierre. On the 6th they were followed by the 1st and 2nd Naval Brigades which marched to positions at Vieux Dieux.

There followed a period of confused fighting with the disorder not helped by a lack of unified command; the Belgian Field Army was commanded by the King of the Belgians while all the fortress garrisons came under the orders of a Belgian Lieut. General. Meanwhile some of the Belgian units were starting to unravel and the R.N.D. fell back to the line of inner forts covering Antwerp from the east and north-east, with Forts 2, 3 and 4 manned by British sailors. By this time the continued defection of Belgian fortress troops left the Division in danger of being encircled and at about 5.30 p.m. on the 8th an order was issued for the British brigades to retire. All three brigades were to rendezvous at Zwyndrecht, a western suburb of Antwerp about 14 miles from centre of the line of forts. This withdrawal, bedevilled by false information and bungled orders, would cost the R.N.D. dearly.

The comedy of errors began when the staff officer charged with the duty of delivering the retirement order passed it only to the commander of Drake Battalion, intimating that the rest of

his brigade had also been notified and was on the point of departure.

Unfortunately this was not the case. The result was that the 2nd and Marine Brigades with Divisional H.Q., plus the Drake Battalion, left immediately as ordered, but the Hawke, Benbow and Collingwood battalions only learned of the retreat at about 9 p.m., and that by accident. Hampered by crowds of refugees from Antwerp the leading units reached Zwyndrecht only to be informed (wrongly) that trains for the coast started from St. Gillaes-Waes, some eight miles further on. The last details, without food or water, eventually reached the station at 3.45 p.m. on the 9th, when they finally entrained for Ostend.

Meanwhile, the Royal Marine rearguard (Portsmouth Battalion) which had taken a different route, arrived at St. Nicholas only to be told (wrongly) that the Germans had already reached Lokeren. The battalion commander decided to march on to Kemseke (one station further down the line from

Left: Maxim-gun squad of the R.N.D. in position before the fall of Antwerp.

168

St. Gillaes) acting on incorrect information from Belgian railway sources that no trains were running from any nearer station. Although the marines were in good order they were encumbered by some 600 stragglers from the naval battalions which they had acquired en route. On the evening of the 9th the party boarded the train, already crowded with Belgian women and children, and set off for the coast. The train had only got as far as Moebeke when, at about 10 p.m., it was derailed and attacked by a German advance party. Major French, battalion commander, later awarded the D.S.O. for his part in the action, rallied his men and although impeded by civilian passengers managed to fight his way clear of the ambush with about half of his force. Many more might have escaped but the majority, woken from a dazed sleep, scrambled out on the far side of the train and into the arms of the waiting Germans. Seven officers and 950 men were captured by a hardly superior enemy force which immediately retreated with its prisoners.

At about the same time the three lagging battalions plus brigade staff, which had started to retreat some four hours after the main body, reached St. Gillaes. Acting on intelligence (later found to be false) from Belgian cavalry that his line of retreat had been cut and the Germans were in front of him, the Commodore and his men turned north. At 10 p.m. on the 9th the party crossed the border into Holland to be interned, rather than surrender to the enemy. However, there were still some stalwarts who were determined to escape. Lieut. Grant R.N.V.R., placed under open arrest for refusing to obey an order, i.e. cross the Dutch border, made his way to Seltzaete on the 10th with 40 Benbow men. Sub Lieut. Modin of the same battalion also brought away a party. Both officers were later awarded the Distinguished Service Cross. The Benbow men seem to have been a determined bunch. Leading Seaman Lockwood, with A/B Seamen Boot and Sawyer, all of Benbow together with Sub. Lieut. Vere Harmsworth of the 1st Brigade staff made their way to the coast and thence to England. Two officers and a petty officer of Hawke Battalion also managed to cross the Channel, via Flushing. In March 1919 on Horse Guards Parade in London when one of the battalions paraded for the last time it was commanded by Commander Lockwood, D.S.O., the same Lockwood who as a leading seaman had avoided internment in 1914. Vere

Harmsworth was not so lucky; he was killed in action on the Somme, in November 1916.

The cost of the Antwerp expedition to the R.N.D. amounted to 238 officers and men, killed, died or wounded, and 39 officers and 2,332 other ranks prisoners of war or interned. Only four members of the Division were later mentioned under the terms of Army Order 193. 5/3303 A.B. Hookham R.N.D. and PO/18644 Pte. Grant R.M.L.I. were each awarded the M.M. for escaping from their respective prisoner of war camps, and Temporary Lieut. Vagg R.N and R/2167 A.B. Rosie were mentioned in despatches for attempting to escape.

Below: Firing line in the R.N.D. Sector at Gallipoli, summer 1915.

When the Division returned to England, having re-embarked at Ostend on the 10th and 11th October, the first priority was to replace the men of the three interned battalions. This was soon accomplished, but the lack of reliable scouts which had imperilled the R.N.D. at Antwerp triggered the idea of establishing a squadron of Naval Divisional Cavalry. However, better sense prevailed and a Divisional Cyclist Company was formed instead.

No doubt the old sweats who had returned from Antwerp hoped that their next military venture would be attended by better luck - but it was not to be. On 28th February 1915 the reinforced Naval Division, clad in khaki instead of blue, sailed from Avonmouth en route to Port Said and Lemnos, their ultimate destination, unknown to them - Gallipoli. The morning of 25th April 1915 saw Anson and Plymouth battalions participate in the six point attack on Cape Helles where the Division's first V.C. was won by Sub Lieut. Tisdall of Anson on 'V' Beach. Tisdall's decoration was not gazetted until 31st March 1916 but by that time, sadly, he was already dead, killed in action on 6th May 1915 at the Second Battle of Krithia.

Further north, the 1st Brigade overshadowed by Australian and New Zealand troops, landed on the southern edge of Gaba Tepe, 'Z' Beach, better known as Anzac Cove. The Division's second V.C. was earned here by a Royal Marine, L/Cpl. Parker of Portsmouth Battalion's medical team, for his gallantry in rescuing the wounded while under fire when he himself had been twice wounded. By 4th May the entire Division was ashore although Anson Battalion was re-embarked for the landing at Suvla Bay on 6th August. By the time the peninsula was evacuated on 8th January 1916 the temporary soldiers had borne their full share of the bitter fighting which had cost the Division 332 officers and 7,198 other ranks as casualties. Of these 128 officers and 2,125 rank and file had been killed or died of wounds. Only two men, both wounded, had been taken prisoner by the Turks.

After leaving the Dardanelles, various battalions and companies of the Division garrisoned the islands of Lemnos, Imbros and Tenedos while the 2nd Brigade saw service on the Salonika front. However, the quiet life ended when the Division landed in France in May 1916 to become part of the B.E.F. Gaps in the ranks caused by Gallipoli casualties had still not been filled and it became necessary to re-deploy the personnel into two brigades (numbered Army fashion) each of four battalions. The

188th Brigade consisted of the 1st and 2nd Royal Marines with the Anson and Howe Battalions, and Hawke, Drake, Hood and Nelson Battalions comprised the 189th Brigade. In order to bring the Division up to infantry strength an army brigade (the 190th) was added and its four battalions were the 1st Honourable Artillery Company, (infantry despite the title) 4th Bedfords, the 7th Royal Fusiliers and the 10th Dublin Fusiliers. This marked the end of a chapter for the Royal Naval Division which now officially became the 63rd (R.N.) Division.

At the end of September 1916, after a period of acclimatization and weapon handling (both the Lewis light machine-gun and Stokes trench mortars were new to the men) the 63rd moved south to take part in one of the closing actions of the Somme offensive, the Battle of the Ancre. The Division's objectives were the fortified village of Beaucourt sur Ancre and the three enemy trenches protecting it, two in front and one immediately behind the village. At 5.45 a.m. on 13th November men of both R.N. brigades scrambled from their jumping off bays and, in spite of heavy casualties, some caused by our own 'shorts,' took the first two German lines. The attack was resumed at 7.45 a.m. on the 14th when the final objectives were taken. On this day another V.C. went to the Division, earned by a future Governor General of New Zealand, Colonel Freyberg. It was awarded for his conspicuous bravery and brilliant leadership, especially on the second day when he was wounded three times while rallying and leading his men. Freyberg had already received the D.S.O. for his gallantry at Gallipoli and he was to earn two bars to that decoration during the remaining months of the war. He would receive yet a third bar to his D.S.O. in Italy in 1945!

The 63rd was relieved on the 16th having taken more prisoners and advanced further than any other division, but at a terrible cost. Casualties in the Naval Brigades alone were not far short of 3,000 officers and men, and the strength of these brigades as they came out of the line was under 600 apiece. Anson alone had lost its C.O., the medical officer and 11 out of 12 of its R.N.V.R. Sub Lieutenants.

In April 1917 the Division entrained for the Arras sector in preparation for yet another offensive which would be officially titled the Second Battle of the Scarpe. On St. George's Day (23rd) at first light as the barrage lifted, nine British Divisions attacked on a nine mile front. The 63rd was on the extreme left of the line with orders to capture the three lines of German trenches in front of the village of Gavrelle, the village itself and the Gavrelle windmill which stood on high ground behind the village. In six days of continual fighting the Division, despite stiff resistance, took all its objectives and beat off numerous German counter-attacks. The men of one platoon continued to hold their portion of captured trench despite thirteen separate such counter-attacks. Needless to say the sailor/soldier attackers paid dearly for their overall success. Later that year the 63rd was switched to the north and on 26th October, in the ghastly Second Battle of Passchendaele, the 1st and 2nd Royal Marines, Howe and Anson Battalions attacked, struggling forward in thigh or waist deep mud, against withering machine-gun and rifle fire. Once again the Division took all its objectives, which were five strongly fortified and garrisoned enemy strong points that dominated the immediate area.

At the end of 1917 the 63rd held the infamous Flesquières Salient which pushed out into enemy lines and was always subjected to marked attention from German artillery, machine-guns and snipers. Just before Christmas, in an action lasting 30 hours, a determined struggle for Welsh Ridge (one of the dominating features in the salient) cost the Division 65 officers and 1,355 men killed, wounded and missing.

Three months later, in the great German Spring offensive of March 1918, the Division continued to hold Flesquières Salient whilst units on its flanks were over-run or destroyed. The 63rd, over 2,000 of the men gassed, then began a fighting retreat until on Sunday, 24th March it tried to hold a position east of Bertincourt, but it was not to be. At 7 a.m. as the British Fifth Army continued to fall back the surviving battalion commanders, in the absence of any contact with higher command, ordered another withdrawal to avoid capture or certain annihilation. As their weary men abandoned the hastily dug trenches they had tried so hard to hold, one was heard to say to his mate, 'It's enough to make you wish you hadn't soddin' well volunteered to go to sea.'

In September 1918, whilst the 63rd was in the forefront of the Battles of the Hindenburg Line, a Victoria Cross was won by W.Z./424 Chief Petty Officer Prowse R.N.V.R. of Drake Battalion, a man who already held the D.C.M. His remarkable citation gazetted 30th October 1918, reads: 'For most conspicuous bravery and devotion to duty. During an advance a portion of his company became disorganised by heavy machine-gun fire from an enemy strong point. Collecting what men were available, he led them with great coolness and bravery against this strong point, capturing it, together with twenty-three prisoners and five machine-guns.

Later he took a patrol forward in face of much enemy opposition and established it on important high ground. On another occasion he displayed great heroism by attacking single-handed an ammunition limber which was trying to recover ammunition, killing three men who accompanied it and capturing the limber.

Two days later he rendered valuable services when covering the advance of his company with a Lewis-gun section, and located later on two machine-gun positions in a concrete emplacement, which were holding up the advance of the battalion on the right. With complete disregard of personal danger, he rushed forward with a small party and attacked and captured these posts, killing six enemy and taking thirteen prisoners and two machine-guns. He was the only survivor of this gallant party, but by this daring and heroic action he enabled the battalion on the right to push forward without further machine-gun fire from the village. Throughout the whole operations his magnificent example and leadership were an inspiration to all, and his courage was superb.' Tragically Prowse never lived to wear his decoration. He was killed in action on 27th September during an attack on the sugar factory at Graincourt.

The Royal Naval Division continued to be heavily involved in the second Battle of Arras, an attempt to seize the northern end of the Hindenburg Line and the Drocourt-Quéant system which lay behind it. In this attack on 2nd September 1918 Sub-Lieut. Harris of Hawke Battalion brought himself to notice by leading his men to capture an enemy machine-gun

Above: Sub-Lt. Joseph Orlando Harris D.S.O., Hawke Bn. R.N.D.

which was holding up the advance of the brigade. Harris, with the unusual Christian names of Joseph Orlando, hailed from Grosvenor Buildings in London's East End where he had worked as a postman. Enlisting in the 8th Bn. City of London Regiment (Post Office Rifles) as no. 2196 he had landed in France on 18th March 1915 and by 21st September 1916 had already been mentioned in despatches as a sergeant. Commissioned on 11th January 1917 he was transferred, with many others, to bolster the R.N.D. which had suffered appalling officer casualties. An unusual man, he had taken the giant step from a postman to an officer and a gentleman, albeit a temporary one.

Hawke Battalion was again in the forefront of the battle on 3rd September 1918, when it cleared the trench system in front of Inchy and moved to within striking distance of the Canal du Nord. At this point the enemy held out until Harris led a party of volunteers who captured the bridgehead after the former postman had personally charged two machine-guns and killed their crews. After this feat it appears that he was recommended for the V.C. but, in the event, he was awarded a D.S.O. - still a rare distinction for a junior officer. His citation, which was not gazetted until 11th January 1919 reads:

'Temporary Sub.-Lt. J.O.Harris, Hawke Bn., R.N.V.R., R.N. Div. For conspicuous gallantry and devotion to duty during an attack. When the advance was checked by heavy machine-gun fire he led his men forward, successfully capturing the machine-gun post and enabling the other companies to advance. Later, he led a party against a bridgehead and captured it, himself charging two machine-gun positions and killing the crews. He set a splendid example of courage and determined leadership.'

On 8th October 1918, in the advance on Cambrai and the last serious engagement fought by Hawke Battalion, the Germans launched a vigorous counter-attack headed by captured British tanks, which was beaten off by the British using German anti-tank guns and rifles which had been taken from the enemy a few minutes earlier! Sadly, Harris never lived to wear his decoration as he was hit during this action and died of wounds two days later. He is buried in Delsaux Farm British Cemetery, Beugny, south of Bapaume. His is the only Naval D.S.O. commemorated on the Post Office Memorial in King Edward's Building, London E.C.

By the end of the war the battle-hardened officers and men of the Royal Naval Division were regarded by the higher command as first-rate infantry, but they continued to regard themselves as sailors. After four and a half years of war they still regulated the time by bells and their N.C.O.s remained petty officers and leading seamen. When they came out of the line they 'went ashore' and their cookhouse remained 'the galley.' As one startled brass hat was heard to remark when invited to 'come aboard,' after stepping into a singularly muddy trench, 'I wish these damn fellas would speak English; still they can certainly fight.' A fitting comment on a fighting Division unequalled by most and surpassed by none

The 63rd (R.N.) Division casualties on the Western Front amounted to 1,683 officers and 34,992 other ranks.

Epilogue

Finally, accounts of two individuals. The first an epic of forti-
tude and the second an epic of endurance.

At 4.30 a.m. on 2nd March 1916 the 8th Battalion, King's Own
(Royal Lancaster Regiment) were to assault the Bluff, a German
strongpoint in the Ypres sector and 'C' Company would lead the
attack. Punctually at zero hour the British barrage shifted onto
the enemy support and reserve positions and officers and men
in the first wave of the leading company scrambled from their
jump-off trench. Among them was Lieut. Reginald Charles
Bowden, one of the many expatriate Britons living in the Argen-
tine who had hastened to England in order to join up as soon
as they could book a passage.

Although Bowden was wounded at the very moment he left
the trench he continued to lead his platoon and refused to
make his way to the regimental aid post. Despite the fact that
his right arm was badly mangled he managed to cut his way
through the enemy wire; at which point he was wounded for
the second time. When he reached the enemy first line a
German infantryman lunged at him with his rifle and
bayonet, but Bowden caught the bayonet in his uninjured left
hand and wrestled with his adversary until the soldier fired
two rounds into his stomach. As he fell forward into the
enemy trench his batman, Private Boyce, came up and killed
the German.

Unable to stand, Bowden insisted on supervising the consolidation of the position until he was satisfied that everything
possible had been done to withstand the expected counter-
attack. Only then did he allow himself to be carried to the rear
and thence to a casualty dressing station.

Bowden died the next day; he was nineteen years of age. His
only decoration is the head stone on his grave in Lijssenhoek
Military Cemetery, Belgium.

The *London Gazette* dated 19th November 1917 announced the award of a D.C.M. to 282496 Private J. Taylor of the 2/4th (City of London Battalion (Royal Fusiliers). A later issue of the *Gazette* on 6th February 1918 carried the citation:

'For conspicuous gallantry and devotion to duty under exceptionally trying and terrible circumstances. Having been cut off with his company he received a bullet in the thigh causing a compound fracture. To avoid capture he crawled into a shell hole, where he remained for a period of over seven weeks, during the whole of which time the surrounding district was subjected to a severe bombardment by our artillery. He subsisted upon tins of bully beef collected at night from dead bodies and water which he obtained in a water-proof cape. After some weeks three of the enemy visited his shell hole, but by feigning death he avoided capture and eventually succeeded in crawling back to our lines - a distance of some nine hundred yards. He displayed extraordinary pluck and endurance by his determination not to fall into the enemy's hands.'

After a long spell in hospital, Taylor, not surprisingly, was discharged medically unfit.

Left: The Western Front - sixty years later - with a German trench and firestep, overgrown, but still clearly marked. Debris includes two sledge carriages from Maxim 1908 heavy machine guns.

Notes on
Campaign Stars and Medals of the Great War

Six different stars and medals were struck for active service in the Great War but only a maximum of three, excluding any decorations for gallantry, could be earned by any one man. There is a rare exception to this rule of three which will be dealt with later.

The first campaign award to be authorised, in August 1917, was the 1914 Star, sometimes incorrectly called the Mons Star, struck in bronze and awarded to personnel who served on the strength of any unit in France or Belgium between 5tht August 1914 and midnight on 22nd/23rd November 1914. Those entitled to the award included civilian doctors and Red Cross workers, nurses, interpreters and chauffeurs. The reverse of the Star is plain and the recipient's number, rank, name and unit are impressed thereon in block capitals. Service in any other land theatre of war, or in any of the 1914 battles and actions fought at sea, did not qualify - much to the disgust of the Royal Navy and others.

In October 1919 a bronze bar to the Star was sanctioned for those who had served under fire, which included shelling by the enemy's mobile artillery, between the same qualifying dates as those for the Star. The bar bore the inscription 5TH AUG-22ND NOV 1914; the last date marking the end of the 1914 Battles of Ypres. Unlike bars to previous medals the clasp has a small hole in each corner to enable it to be sewn directly onto the ribbon. A small silver rosette takes the place of the bar when only ribbons, and not medals, are worn.

The 1914-15 Star was authorised in 1918 and is identical to the 1914 Star except that the months have been removed and the centre scroll bears the dates 1914-15 instead of 1914. It was awarded to all those in any theatre of war between 5th August 1914 and 31st December 1915, including the North-West Frontier of India in 1915, but not to those who only saw service for which the Africa General Service or

Left: 1914 Star with bar.

Above: 1914–15 Star.

Sudan medal was granted. The ribbon, red, white and blue, shaded and watered, is the same as that for the 1914 Star. Recipients of the latter were not eligible for the 1914-15 Star.

The British War Medal, struck in silver, carries the dates 1914-1918 but could be earned up to 1920 for certain post-war operations, chiefly mine clearance at sea and service in North and South Russia, the Eastern Baltic, Siberia, Black Sea and the Caspian. Over five and a half million of these medals were issued, and just over 100,000 in bronze were awarded to members of various native Labour contingents. The obverse carries the coinage head of King George V and the reverse of the medal shows St. George on horseback trampling the shield of the Central Powers. Underneath is a skull and crossbones, the symbol of death, and above is the risen sun of victory. The ribbon has a watered broad orange centre flanked on each side by white, black and blue stripes.

An Allied Victory Medal was awarded to all personnel who qualified for either of the stars and, with a few exceptions, to holders of the British War Medal. The first issues were finished in dull bronze, but later issues, which are by far the

The British War Medal.

Left: Obverse.

Above: Reverse.

majority, were gilded. The obverse shows the winged, standing figure of Victory with a palm branch in her right hand, while the reverse carries the inscription THE GREAT WAR FOR CIVILIZATION 1914-1919. Once again the dates on the medal have nothing in common with the actual qualifying dates. The ribbon is rainbow patterned with red, yellow, green, blue and violet, working from the centre outwards. Those individuals who were mentioned in despatches wore a bronze oakleaf on the ribbon of this medal.

A bronze Mercantile Marine War Medal was issued by the Board of Trade to members of the Merchant Navy for at least one voyage in a danger zone or six months at sea under certain named conditions, principally service on lightships or pilot vessels. The reverse shows the bows of a merchant steamer ploughing through a heavy sea, with a sailing ship in the background and a sinking U-boat in the right foreground. In the exergue in three lines appears FOR WAR SERVICE MERCANTILE MARINE 1914-1918. The obverse carries the coinage head of King George V, similar to the British War Medal. The ribbon is watered green and red separated by a

The Victory Medal.

Left: Obverse with Mention in Despatches oakleaf emblem on ribbon.

Above: Reverse.

narrow white stripe down the centre, and the colours are supposed to indicate the port, starboard and steaming lights of a ship. Only the holder's name appears on the edge. Recipients of the Mercantile Marine Medal automatically qualified for the British War Medal.

An exception to the rule of three mentioned in the first paragraph is the case of a serviceman who earned his Star, War and Victory medals before being wounded in such a manner as to preclude further service as a soldier or sailor, but joined the Merchant Navy and qualified for the Mercantile Marine Medal. Such groups of four exist, but they are rare.

A bronze Territorial Force War Medal was authorised in April 1920 for members of the T.F. and T.F. Nursing Service who volunteered for service overseas on or before 30th September 1914, but did not actually serve overseas in time to qualify for either of the Stars, although they did have to serve overseas at some time in order to qualify for the medal.

Above: The Mercantile Marine Medal (reverse).

Above right: Territorial Force War Medal (obverse)

Recipients of a Star could not qualify for this medal. The ribbon is watered yellow with two green stripes, each 4_ mms wide and a similar distance from each edge.

Representations were made by the Governments of Australia and New Zealand for a Gallipoli Star as an award to their servicemen who had fought, and in many cases died, in that theatre of war. The proposal was turned down on the grounds that a separate medal for the ANZAC troops would have been unfair to the British, Indian and other troops who had also served in the peninsula. Survivors and their next of kin had to be content with the 1914-15 Star.

In 1919 separate naval and military committees sat to consider the question or battle bars for the British War Medal. Their deliberations recommended 68 clasps for the Royal Navy and 94 for the Army, of which 44 were for actions on the Western Front. No one man was to sport more than nine bars. However, the idea was finally shelved on the grounds of cost, although the naval proposals had already been approved by the King and printed in an Admiralty Order in 1920.

This decision not to award battle bars meant that it was impossible to evaluate a man's service by looking at his medals. For example, a soldier who strayed over the frontier into Holland in 1914, probably through no fault of his own, then spent a very comfortable war as an internee safe from bombs and bullets and was even allowed home leave to the U.K. Compare this existence with the experience of Private Frank Richards (author of *Old Soldiers Never Die*) a reservist recalled to the 2nd Battalion Royal Welch Fusiliers, who landed in France on 11th August 1914 and served on the Western Front until 11th November 1918. Both men would have worn identical campaign medals, viz. 1914 Star and bar, British War and Victory Medals.

Above: Territorial Force War Medal (reverse).

Consider also a man in the 2nd Battalion The King's Own who landed with his battalion in France on 18th January 1916, just too late to qualify for the 1914-15 Star. He would spend the next three years, if he survived, in bloody trench warfare and earn the British War and Victory Medals. Those two medals would also be awarded to a member of the 34th (County of London) Battalion who went into the line late in August 1918. Three years or three months earned the same campaign medals. Only the man who wears the medal knows what it is worth.

Generally speaking, the 1914-15 Star, War & Victory trio, or the War and Victory pair, known respectively as Pip, Squeak and Wilfred or, in the case of the pair, Mutt and Jeff, after popular cartoon characters of the period, were not highly regarded by the rank and file. During the post-war depression pawnbrokers' windows were full of these medals which had been struck to commemorate some of the bloodiest battles ever fought by British troops. They were pledged, and rarely redeemed, for the scrap silver value of the British War Medals which was half a crown, or 12½p in our modern debased currency. Happily, the 1914 Star and bar trio tended to be held in much higher esteem by the holder.

Medals of the dead were sent, together with a bronze memorial plaque bearing the full names of the deceased, to their next of kin.

Decorations

Victoria Cross (V.C.). Britain's highest award for bravery which was instituted 29th January 1856. During the period 1914-1920, 415 V.C.s and two bars (both to medical officers) were awarded, which included Allied post-war intervention in North and South Russia.

Distinguished Service Order (D.S.O.). An officers decoration which could be awarded for meritorious or distinguished service as well as gallantry in action. When awarded to a subaltern it was invariably for bravery.

Military Cross (M.C.). Instituted 28th December 1914 and confined to junior officers and warrant officers for gallantry in action. From 1914-1920 there were 37,081 awards with 2983 first bars, 168 second bars and four third bars for service in the field. In addition, there were 23 M.C.s, with one first and one second bar for services in connection with the war. These last would include awards in connection with air raids, etc.

Distinguished Conduct Medal (D.C.M.). Came into being on 4th December 1854 during the Crimean War and was awarded to other ranks only - the second highest gallantry award after the V.C. From 1914-1920 there were 24,620 awards with 472 first bars and nine second bars.

Military Medal (M.M.). Other rank award for bravery in the field instituted in March 1916 (without provision for retrospective awards). Like the M.C. for officers, it fulfilled a role in the award system as widespread distribution of the D.C.M. would have devalued the exclusivity of that award. 115,589 medals issued during 1914-1920, with 5796 first bars, 180 second bars and one third bar.

Meritorious Service Medal (M.S.M.). From its institution in 1854 until 1916 this medal had been a reward for soldiers above the rank of corporal. However, by 1916 it was obvious there was a need for a military award to recognise acts of gallantry other than those performed in action. Accordingly, by a Royal Warrant of 4th October 1916 eligibility for the medal was extended to 'warrant officers, non-commissioned officers and men, who render valuable and meritorious service.' For valuable services during the period 1916-1920, 21,427 M.S.M.s were awarded; for gallantry during the same period 350, and for devotion to duty, 143.

Mention in Despatches. Confined to officers until 2nd March 1843 when, for the first time, other ranks were mentioned by Sir Charles Napier in his Scinde campaign dispatch. However, there was no visible mark of the distinction borne on the uniform until January 1920 when King George V approved the design of a multi-leaved bronze oak leaf to be worn on the ribbon of the Victory Medal. Irrespective of the number of mentions gained by an individual only one oak leaf was won. 141,082 military mentions gazetted for the period 1914-1920.

As far as decorations generally were concerned, in the early years of the war a number of bravery awards were made to officers and men who were not under fire, and nowhere near the front line. Hence in 1916 a committee sat and seriously considered whether gallantry awards for service behind the lines should not have a different ribbon to those earned in the trenches! In any case it should be noted that from April 1917 onwards in France and Flanders the Commander-in-Chief was empowered to award *each month*, 200 D.S.O.s and 500 M.C.s, in addition to D.C.M.s, M.M.s and M.S.M.s *without limit*.

Glossary

ANZAC: Australian and New Zealand Army Corps.

B.E.F.: British Expeditionary Force.

British Infantry Formations

Army: Strength variable; usually two or three Corps.

Corps: Usually two or three Divisions.

Division: In 1914 a British infantry division comprised three brigades, each of four battalions, with two Maxim machine-guns per battalion. Divisional artillery consisted of three brigades of 18-pounders - 54 field guns in all, plus one field Howitzer brigade - eighteen 4.5" howitzers, and one heavy battery - four 60-pdrs; plus support services and divisional troops. There were several changes during the war and by the end of hostilities a division consisted of three infantry brigades each of three battalions, with 36 Lewis (light) machine-guns to each battalion - totalling 324. Each brigade included a light trench mortar battery of eight 3" Stokes trench mortars - or 24 per division. Vickers belt-fed heavy machine-guns were concentrated into a divisional machine-gun battalion of four companies, each with 16 guns - 64 all told. Plus increased artillery and support services.

Battalion: H.Q. and four rifle companies with an official strength of six officers and 221 other ranks to each, plus six officers and 93 men (including the machine-gun section) for Battalion H.Q.

Company: Four platoons and a company H.Q.

Platoon: Four sections, each of one N.C.O. and up to ten men, plus a platoon HQ consisting of a subaltern, platoon sergeant, two runners and sometimes a signaller. By the end of the war each platoon had its own two-man Lewis gun section (more if they could be scrounged).

Bomber. After First Ypres, when manufactured hand grenades became available, a certain number of men in each battalion were trained to use them and were given the name of grenadiers. The Grenadier Guards objected, claiming an exclusive right to the name as having been specially conferred on them after Waterloo to commemorate their part in defeating Napoleon's Grenadiers of the Guard. According to Sir Frederick Ponsonby in *The History of the Grenadier Guards in the Great War* the Guards considered it 'an infringement of their privileges and misleading.' In the event the Colonel of the 1st Battalion, Grenadier Guards, protested to the War Office against the 'usurpation' of the name. After a lengthy controversy a final appeal was made to the King and in May 1916 its was officially announced that at His Majesty's 'express wish' the description 'bomber' should be substituted for that of 'grenadier.'

C.O.: Commanding Officer.

C.Q.M.S.: Company Quarter Master Sergeant.

C.S.M.: Company Sergeant Major. A Warrant Officer Class II.

Grubber: Slang word for an individual entrenching spade fitted with a shaft too short for serious digging but long enough to be a nuisance, especially going over the top. Generally regarded as useless weight by the troops and discarded whenever possible; hence the surprising numbers reported as 'destroyed by enemy action.'

G.S.O.: General Staff Officer.

H.Q.: Headquarters.

In the air: Flank(s) not covered by friendly troops.

Jaeger: German rifleman.

Kitchener's New Armies: Battalions raised in response to the famous appeal on posters, featuring Field Marshal Kitchener with the legend YOUR COUNTRY NEEDS YOU. Popularly known as Kitchener's Mob.

Leap frogging: Term for a form of attack introduced in 1917 for penetrating an enemy trench system, whereby successive limits were given to successive waves of infantry. Once the first wave captured its allotted objective it consolidated as the subsequent wave passed through and beyond it, or in other words leap frogged forward to take the next objective ahead. An artillery barrage lifted and cleared the way for each advancing wave of infantry. It always worked well on paper.

L.G.: London Gazette.

L. of C.: Lines of Communication.

Minenwerfer: German trench mortar. Several calibres in use

ranging from a lightweight, firing a 7.6cm (3_ inch) bomb to a heavy mortar throwing a 24.5cm (9_ inch) projectile.

No-Man's-Land: The strip of open ground, albeit littered with dead bodies, barbed wire and the debris of war, between the opposing trenches. On the Western Front No-Man's-Land varied in width from only a few yards in places to a quarter of a mile or more. The term was apparently coined by a journalist and first appeared in print on 15th September 1914.

N.C.O.: Non-commissioned officer; colour sergeant, sergeant, corporal; or lance corporal. The latter was an appointment and not a rank.

Over the Top (or Over the Bags): Leaving the trenches to attack - going over the sandbags towards the German positions.

Pickelhaube: German peace-time helmet worn in action until the introduction of the 'coal scuttle' type steel helmet. A popular and desirable souvenir, but dangerous as those left behind in evacuated dugouts were often booby-trapped.

Pill Box: German ferro-concrete battlefield redoubts, sometimes circular in shape (hence the name). Used from the autumn of 1917 onwards to defend sections of the line in Flanders and manned by small detachments of infantry with machine-guns. Proof against all but a direct hit by the heaviest artillery.

R.S.M.: Regimental Sergeant Major, a Warrant Officer class I.

Strengths: The *official strength* of a British infantry battalion was 30 officers and 977 men, or 1007 all ranks, but this figure was never maintained once the unit was in action. *Ration strength* was different again and excluded all those officers and men who were away from the battalion, either on courses, of which there were many - signalling, bombing, sniping etc. - or in hospital or convalescent or lucky enough to be on leave. Finally there was *trench strength* which was the actual number of combatants in the firing line, but this was not the whole of the ration strength. By late 1916, when the unit was to go over the top, a cadre of officers, N.C.O.s and men was left behind out of the line (known as L.O.B. or Left Out of Battle). This cadre was then available to reconstitute the battalion if - or more often when - it suffered heavy casualties.

Storm Troops (German *Sturm Truppen*): Special formations of picked troops, all young, bachelors or married men without children, used to spearhead a general attack. First employed at Verdun in 1916. Led by specially trained officers and N.C.O.s, each assault squad mustered about 100 men plus bombers, machine-gunners and flame-thrower operatives.

Swords, infantry: It is surprising that officers still carried swords in action for the first year of the war. One of the best examples of the futility of the sword in modern warfare comes from the pen of Field Marshal Montgomery, describing his experience as a subaltern attacking the enemy-held village of Meteren on 13th October 1914: "When Zero arrived I drew my newly sharpened sword and shouted to my platoon to follow me, which it did. We charged forward... as we neared the objective I suddenly saw in front of me a trench full of Germans, one of whom was aiming his rifle at me.

In my training as a young officer I had received much instruction in how to kill my enemy with a bayonet fixed to a rifle... Indeed I had been considered good on the bayonet-fighting course against sacks filled with straw, and had won prizes in man-to-man contents in the gymnasium. But now I had no rifle and bayonet; I had only a sharp sword, and I was confronted by a large German who was about to shoot me. In all my short career in the Army no one had taught me how to kill a German with a sword. The only sword exercise I knew was saluting drill, learnt under a sergeant-major on the barrack square.

An immediate decision was clearly vital. I hurled myself through the air at the German and kicked him as hard as I could in the lower part of the stomach; the blow was well aimed at a tender spot. I had read much about the value of surprise in war. There is no doubt that the German was surprised and it must have seemed to him a new form of war; he fell to the ground in great pain and I took my first prisoner!"

Bibliography

Regimental and Battalion Histories

A.I.F., 14th Battalion. N.Wanliss. Australia 1929.

Black Watch (Royal Highlanders), Vol. III. Ed. by Major-General A.G.Wauchope. London 1926.

10th Canadian Infantry Battalion. Daniel G.Dancocks. Alberta, Canada 1990.

Cheshire Regiment. H.Crookenden. Chester 1938.

Cheshire Regiment: The 1st Bn. at Mons and the Miniature Colour. F.Simpson. Chester 1929.

Devonshire Regiment. C.T.Atkinson. Exeter 1926.

Diex Aïx (Royal Guernsey Light Infantry). Major Edwin Parkes. Guernsey. 1992.

East Surrey Regiment, Vol. II. Col. H.W.Pearse and Brig.-Gen. H.S.Sloman. London 1933.

Essex Regiment, Vol. VI. John W.Burrows. Southend 1935.

Grenadier Guards, Vol. III. Lt.-Col. Sir Frederick Ponsonby. London 1920.

Hawke Battalion, R.N.D. Douglas Jerrold. London 1925.

King's Own Yorkshire Light Infantry, Vol. III. Lt.-Col. R.C.Bond. London 1930 & Vol. IV. Gen. Sir Charles Deedes. London 1946.

King's Own Scottish Borderers. Capt. S.Gillon. London 1930.

Lincolnshire Regiment. Ed. by Major-Gen. C.R.Simpson. London 1931.

London Scottish. Lt.-Col. J.H.Lindsay. London 1925.

Manchester Regiment, 16th, 17th, 18th & 19th Battalions. Manchester 1923.

2nd Munsters in France. Lt.-Col. H.S.Jervis. Aldershot 1922.

Prince of Wales Volunteers (South Lancashire). Capt. H.Whalley-Kelly. Aldershot. 1935.

Rifle Brigade Vol. I. Capt. R.C.Berkeley. London 1927.

Rifle Brigade Chronicle 1926. Ed. by Major H.G.Parkyn. London 1927.

Royal Marines: Britain's Sea Soldiers, Vol. III. Col. Sir H.E.Blumberg. Devonport 1927.
Royal Munster Fusiliers 1861-1922. Capt. S.McCance. Aldershot. 1927.
Royal Naval Division. Douglas Jerrold. London 1923.
Royal Welch Fusiliers, Vol. III. Major C.H.Dudley-Ward. London 1928.
Suffolk Regiment. Lt.-Col. C.C.R.Murphy. London 1928.
2nd Wiltshire Regiment. Major W.S.Shepherd. Aldershot 1927.

Other works
The ANZACs, Patsy Adam-Smith. London 1978.
Armageddon Road, Ed. by Terry Norman. London 1982.
The Bond of Sacrifice, Ed. Col. L.A.Clutterbuck. London, contemp.
British Campaign Medals, Robert W.Gould. London 1994.
Cheerful Sacrifice, Arras 1917, Jonathan Nicholls. London 1990.
Gallipoli, The Fading Vision, John North. London 1936.
The Great War: A History, F.A.Mumby. London, contemp.
The Guards Division in the Great War, Lt.-Col. C.Headlam. London 1924.
The Kaiser's Battle, Martin Middlebrook. London 1978.
Locations of British Cavalry, Infantry & Machine Gun Units, 1914-1924, Robert W.Gould. London 1977.
London Gazette. Various dates.
Machine Gunner 1914-1918, C.E.Crutchley. London 1975.
Memoirs, FM Montgomery of Alamein. London 1956.
Officers Died in the Great War, HMSO 1919.
Official History of the War, Brig.-Gen. J.E.Edmonds et al. London 1921-1948. Various volumes.
Soldiers Died in the Great War, HMSO 1921 and 1922.
V.C.s of the First World War, Gallipoli, S.Snelling. London 1995.